FILIPINOS REPRESENT

FILIPINOS REPRESENT

*DJs, Racial Authenticity, and the
Hip-hop Nation*

Antonio T. Tiongson Jr.

University of Minnesota Press

Minneapolis

London

An earlier version of chapter 4 was previously published as "Claiming Hip Hop: Authenticity Debates, Filipino DJs, and Contemporary U.S. Racial Formations," in Martin Japtok and Rafiki Jenkins, eds., *Authentic Blackness / "Real" Blackness* (New York: Peter Lang Publishing, Inc., 2011), 85–100.

Published by the University of Minnesota Press
111 Third Avenue South, Suite 290
Minneapolis, MN 55401–2520
http://www.upress.umn.edu

Library of Congress Cataloging-in-Publication Data

Tiongson, Antonio T.
  Filipinos represent : DJs, racial authenticity, and the hip-hop nation / Antonio T. Tiongson Jr.
  Includes bibliographical references and index.
  ISBN 978-0-8166-7938-6 (hc : alk. paper)
  ISBN 978-0-8166-7939-3 (pb : alk. paper)
  1. Popular culture. 2. Popular culture—United States—21st century.
3. Hip-hop—United States. 4. Filipino Americans—Ethnic identity.
5. United States—Race relations. 6. Racism—United States. I. Title.
  HM621.T586 2013
  305.899'21073—dc23

                                    2013010523

Printed in the United States of America on acid-free paper

The University of Minnesota is an equal-opportunity educator and employer.

20 19 18 17 16 15 14 13   10 9 8 7 6 5 4 3 2 1

Contents

Acknowledgments

First and foremost, I want to thank my mother—affectionately known as "Malou" to her friends—for her steadfast love and support at every stage of my career in academia. This book is dedicated to her. I also want to acknowledge Mian, Papa (R.I.P.), Tita Lil, Tito Fred, and the Ramos and Cunanan families for their support through the years, as well as Lucee for all the love and joy she has given me.

Two individuals in particular deserve special mention for their exemplary mentorship, unwavering support, and deep friendship. I first met Rick Bonus as a first-year graduate student at the University of California, San Diego, and he has proven to be an inimitable mentor and dear friend ever since. He provided steadfast support during the early stages of my graduate career, which proved to be crucial in terms of my development as a scholar, and he continues to do so as I advance in my academic career. I especially want to thank Rick for easing my transition into graduate school, modeling the nuances of teaching, and teaching me the broader significance and relevance of the study of Filipinos. I am also greatly indebted to Dylan Rodriguez, who has proven to be indispensable to my intellectual and political development. I especially appreciate his professional and emotional support through the years, and his display of what it means to do critically rigorous and politically engaged scholarship. I am most thankful for Dylan's generosity with his time and for his deep commitment to the success of junior faculty like me. In addition, I want to acknowledge Jane Rhodes, who played an instrumental role in my graduate career at UCSD and who continued to play an important role in my career trajectory.

Thanks also to the editors and staff at University of Minnesota Press. I want to especially thank Richard Morrison and Erin Warholm-Wohlenhaus for their professionalism and tireless efforts in helping bring the project into fruition. It has been a pleasure and privilege working with both of you.

I want to acknowledge colleagues that I have had the pleasure to interact with and befriend through my various stops at several academic institutions. I want to express my gratitude to colleagues at Mount Holyoke College for creating such a supportive and intellectually nurturing environment: Don Weber, Simone Davis, Anthony Lee, and Cynthia Meehan. I want to especially thank Iyko Day for being such a model colleague and friend. I also appreciate the relationships I cultivated at Colorado College: Mario Montano, Alberto Hernandez-Lemus, Emily Chan, Anne Hyde, Sandra Wong, Adrienne Seward, Laura Padilla, Eric Perramond, Doug Monroy, Eric Popkin, Victor Cisneros, Murphy Brausel, and Suzanne Ridings. I also want to thank Nila Bhattacharjya, Zelideth Rivas, Shannon Mason, and Ronak Kapadia for their comradeship during my stay in Colorado. Additionally, I want to acknowledge the Department of Ethnic Studies at the University of Colorado at Boulder for serving as my intellectual home in Colorado. Thanks in particular to Danika Medak-Saltzman for being a dear friend and an exemplary colleague. I especially appreciate her unwavering support during a tumultuous time at Colorado College, her always astute commentary on my work, and for introducing me to Lucee.

Most recently, my career trajectory has taken me to the Department of American Studies at the University of New Mexico. I want to thank my colleagues for creating such a welcoming and supportive environment: Alyosha Goldstein, Rebecca Schreiber, A. Gabriel Melendez, Michael L. Trujillo, Shante Paradigm Smalls, Amy L. Brandzel, David Correia, Jennifer Nez Denetdale, Alex Lubin, Irene Vasquez, Katie Holscher, and Gerald Vizenor. I look forward to working with all of you in the years to come. I truly feel blessed to be part of such a dynamic and reputable program. I also want to acknowledge Barbara Reyes for her support and encouragement when we were both at UCSD and her continued support and encouragement now that we are both at UNM. Moreover, I want to thank the graduate students for the warm reception. I look forward to working with you and serving as a resource. I have been fortunate to work with outstanding staff assistants throughout my career and once again, I am fortunate to work with Sandy Rodrigue, who is such an individual.

I also want to acknowledge the community of Pinoy and Pinay scholars whom I am honored to call both friends and colleagues. I am especially appreciative of all that I have learned from this cohort of scholars about the workings of empire, the significance of culture, and the challenges and complexities of comparative work: Robyn Rodriguez, Nerissa S. Balce, Lucy Burns, Dean Saranillio, Linda Espana-Maram, Rudy Guevarra Jr., Jeff Santa Ana, and Allan Isaac. I want to send special acknowledgments to Martin Manalansan for his exemplary mentorship. Additionally, I want to acknowledge a cohort of scholars who have been generous with their time and insights at various points in my career: Lisa Lowe, Lisa Park, Michael Omi, Cathy Schlund-Vials, and Victor Viesca. I want to thank Anita Mannur and Theo Gonzalvez in particular for their careful reading of the manuscript and insightful comments that greatly enhanced it.

Moreover, I want to acknowledge a group of guys in the Bay Area for our daily sessions at "HQ": Brian Sales, Frank Ramos, Jose Santiago, Tito Marinez, Amancio "Jojo" Liangco, Perry Rodriguez, Noli Agustin, Waldo Achacoso, Mel Ferrer, and Ricky Ramos. I thank you for the conversation, camaraderie, and "insights" on the human condition. Additionally, I want to recognize Edgardo Gutierrez and Ricardo Gutierrez, who coedited *Positively No Filipinos Allowed* along with me and who continue to be part of my support network in the Bay Area. I also want to thank the San Francisco Giants for 2010 and 2012 and ending the misery of all Giants fans. Finally, I want to thank my respondents for making this book possible.

Introduction   Claiming Hip-hop

ON SEPTEMBER 7, 1997, the International Turntablist Federation (ITF) held its second annual World Championships at the Palace of Fine Arts in San Francisco in various skill categories: scratching, beat juggling, team or DJ bands, and best all around.[1] In all these categories, Filipino DJs made up the bulk of the competitors, prompting the host to remind the audience that even though Filipinos dominate DJ competitions across the nation and the globe, ITF actually does not stand for "It's Totally Filipinos." This elicited laughter from the crowd, which also largely comprised Filipino youth in their teens and early twenties.

As the host's comments indicate, DJing has become an expressive form in which many Filipino youth invest their time, energy, and passion. By the 1980s, Filipino youth had come to dominate the local DJ scene in places like San Francisco and the Bay Area, Los Angeles, and New York, subsequently making their mark nationally not only as battle DJs but also as club DJs, and radio DJs in an expressive form historically associated with African Americans. This phenomenon has international dimensions as well with Filipino DJs from Canada and Australia winning competitions and both success and acclaim.[2] The crowd's response, therefore, was not a surprise given the emergence of DJing as a signifier of Filipino youth identity and the now commonplace assumption that Filipinos make the best DJs in the world.

In highlighting the dominance of Filipino youth in DJ culture, the host that night spoke to how DJing has become a constituent element of Filipino youth identities and cultural practices. At the same time, however, he touched on a set of issues that will be addressed in this study, issues having to do with the contours of contemporary youth culture, politics, and identity and more broadly, the configurations of U.S. racial formations and global diasporic formations in the post–civil rights era. For example, what is the nature of Filipino youth involvement with DJing? What forms of identification and affiliation are made possible through Filipino youth involvement in DJing? What kinds of narratives underlie their cultural claims? How do Filipino youth go about explaining their involvement in DJing? What does it mean for Filipino youth to not only dominate an expressive form historically associated with African Americans but also claim it as their own? How do these kinds of claims complicate hip-hop's status as an "African American thing"?[3]

Answers to these questions are also telling because of what they suggest about the perceived boundaries of Filipinoness and the subsequent questions that arise. Does an embrace of DJing signify or represent a "loss of culture" or a "loss of tradition," or more to the point, an indicator of a lack of Filipinoness? Why do U.S.-based Filipino youth rely on this expressive form to express their Filipinoness, an expressive form seemingly far removed from practices considered Filipino rather than on conventional markers of Filipino culture?[4] What are the implications for the perceived boundaries of Filipinoness? Given the highly masculinist orientation of DJ culture, what does Filipino youth involvement in DJing suggest about the ways ethnicity and gender collude with one another to define the boundaries of Filipinoness? How is DJing implicated in the formation of gendered subjectivities and meanings, including formations of femininity and masculinity among Filipino youth?

In *Filipinos Represent*, I interrogate those complex forms of identification taking place among Filipino DJs and what they reveal about the dynamics of U.S. racial formations and global diasporic formations. I delineate the complexities (and contradictions) of the current cultural terrain occupied by Filipino youth, a cultural terrain characterized by competing agendas and conflicting visions of Filipinoness that only makes sense "via the American racial classification system but also via identifications (good, bad, or ambivalent) with other Filipino translocal communities."[5] The aim is to provide a fuller account of the contexts in which Filipino youth involvement within hip-hop takes place—one that takes seriously the specificities of group racialization and diasporic histories—as a way to illuminate contemporary racial formations and clarify current configurations of diasporic identity and culture.

In this book, I seek to illuminate the contours and trajectory of contemporary U.S. racial formations and discourses in the post–civil rights era through a consideration of how issues of cultural ownership, origins, and authenticity play out within hip-hop. I argue that in many ways, the terms by which this debate has taken place is symptomatic of contemporary racial discourse— the tendency to conceive of race and cultural ownership either in narrow, exclusive terms in which there seems to be no room to account for varied origins and influences or in liberal, pluralist terms in which "difference" no longer makes a difference.

While the bulk of recent hip-hop scholarship has aimed to detach the genre from any exclusive association with African Americanness, this body of work has yet to adequately scrutinize the broader theoretical and political implications of doing so. As such, this book constitutes a critical engagement with not just the shifting parameters of Filipinoness but also that of blackness. More specifically, it aims to explore what is at stake when blackness is invoked either as a way to claim culture or problematize claims of cultural ownership (typically through charges of essentialism). I am particularly interested in addressing the following questions: Why is there a seeming injunction to dissociate hip-hop with blackness, on what basis, and why now? What is being accomplished socially, politically, and discursively with the disavowal of blackness? Despite the exponential increase of scholarship in recent years, these and other related questions have received relatively little attention from scholars in the emerging field of hip-hop studies. These questions, in other words, have yet to be worked through in a sustained manner. Instead, a recurrent theme is the deracialization of hip-hop, which I argue is symptomatic of contemporary racial discourse and, in particular, the inability to think about race in a critically sustained way in the contemporary moment.

Filipinos Represent also aims to advance our understanding of the workings of diaspora, which has become an important category of analysis in various disciplines in both the humanities and the social sciences. This study strives to reconfigure standard diasporic accounts predicated largely on the experiences of the immigrant or first generation and on a particular set of activities through a critical consideration of youth cultural productions within the context of the Filipino diaspora. Instead, by centering the experiences of second-generation Filipino Americans, this study attempts to provide a more nuanced account of the complex forms of identification generated in the diaspora that complicate and confound the normative boundaries of Filipino identity and culture. More specifically, it aims to foreground the different means by which Filipino youth go about forging cultural affiliations that are not simply oriented toward the homeland. What it means to be Filipino, therefore, cannot be reduced to conventional markers of Filipinoness. Rather, Filipino youth involvement in DJing is emblematic of the need to reconceptualize in broad terms the contours of Filipino diasporic identity and culture.[6]

Critical Engagements, Critical Considerations

Filipinos Represent represents a critical engagement with what is now a fairly substantial body of writing that has come to be categorized under the rubric of "hip-hop studies." It constitutes a critical engagement with the emergent themes in this burgeoning body of work, what can be described as the "multiracial, multicultural, and multilingual" turn in the literature.[7] More recent literature has sought to complicate and broaden the ground from which to consider the racial scope of hip-hop, long considered to be an African American expressive form, and in particular, questions of cultural belonging and entitlement that hitherto have been generally perceived as underwritten by blackness. A recurrent theme in the literature is that it can no longer be assumed that hip-hop is an exclusively African American expressive form or that it is simply a signifier of blackness given the formative role that other racialized groups and their attendant cultural practices and traditions have played in its evolution and given hip-hop's popularity on a global scale. A prevailing theme is that blackness can no longer be considered the sole guarantor of authenticity or viewed as the only "true" source of authenticity.

This recent turn in the literature, however, has proven to be a point of contention, a major fault line that has generated a great deal of debate and discussion. In the pages that follow, I attempt to make sense of the broader implications—both theoretical and political—of this recent turn in hip-hop literature through a consideration of the ways in which knowledge of the culture is constructed, framed, and conveyed around questions of cultural origins, belonging, and authenticity, and the ways in which a group of nonblack youth go about carving out a niche in a cultural form historically associated with African Americans. I make the case that while it is indeed the case that hip-hop has not only become multicultural but also global in terms of its scope and appeal and therefore cannot be simply viewed as an expression of African Americanness, it does not follow (and is just as problematic) that hip-hop has also become an "an all-purpose-thing, of equal utility and relevance to anyone, anywhere, as long as you're 'with it.'"[8]

To conceive of hip-hop as such fails to do justice to the complexities of power relations among racialized groups and the subtle and intricate ways in which power relations structure the involvement of various groups of youth. Instead, in such readings of hip-hop, questions of power and structure are collapsed into questions of cross-cultural appeal and understanding. To borrow from Jacqueline Urla, "appropriations and border crossings are always inflected by histories of power that shape when cultural, ethnic, or linguistic boundaries are asserted, when they are transgressed, and they are misunderstood."[9] It is precisely these "histories of power" that are overlooked in recent scholarship on hip-hop, histories of power that condition and shape the participation of different groups of youth in hip-hop, histories of power that I seek to interrogate in this study. This body of work, for example, has yet to address the following questions in a critically sustained manner. What does it mean to conceive of hip-hop as a multicultural and global expressive form? Does it mean that any group or all groups have the same kind of claim to hip-hop? Who gets to adjudicate these claims and on what basis? Instead, I make the argument that as a whole, the literature has yet to substantively address questions of race, culture, and power and relations among them.

It is not my interest, therefore, to reinscribe the experience of Filipino youth into standard accounts of hip-hop in a celebratory or additive manner with the aim of providing a corrective to conventional hip-hop historiography that hitherto elided the contributions of particular groups. By the same token, I do not set out to provide a historical account of Filipino youth involvement in DJ culture or a direct analysis of why such a high concentration of Filipino youth are into DJing. Going against the grain of extant hip-hop scholarship, I am also not interested in delineating the resistive aspects of hip-hop or tracing its broadening scope through the documentation of the involvement of yet another group.

Rather, I provide an analysis of the kinds of claims made in the name of "culture"—what serves as the basis for these claims, what is being accomplished through the deployment of culture, and the stakes—in a way that accounts for the contingencies of power and history. I make an effort to interrogate what Virginia R. Dominguez has described as "the seeming transparency of the reference to culture"[10] and the implications for the theorization of racial and diasporic formations. I am especially interested in how study participants conceive of questions of cultural origins, ownership, and legitimacy.

I focus on hip-hop because of the way it has become a key site over which competing claims of cultural ownership, race, and authenticity are made. Given its history, racialization, and representation, hip-hop constitutes an ideal space to explore the varied articulations of race in the contemporary moment. As R. Scott Heath remarks, "hip-hop culture is intricately linked to any comprehensive understanding of race and national identity in the U.S. at the turn of the 21st century."[11] More broadly, hip-hop constitutes a critically important site for analyzing the processes of racialization—how social subjects position themselves and are positioned as racial(ized) subjects.

I focus in particular on DJing because this element of hip-hop has emerged as a key site for exploring the shifting boundaries of Filipinoness given the dominance of Filipino youth in this expressive form. It constitutes a strategic locus where contemporary discourses of Filipinoness are generated, struggled over, and elaborated with reference to a larger narrative of race and migration at the same time that it provides specific possibilities for Filipino youth to creatively reimagine individual and group identities. DJing, therefore, provides a prism with which to make sense of how Filipinoness functions at this contemporary moment as well as the dynamics of contemporary Filipino cultural politics.

In placing race at the center of critical analysis, *Filipinos Represent* engages with the field of comparative race studies and, in particular, the comparative turn in the study of race and ethnicity. In this body of work, a focal point is making sense of the racialization process through a comparative lens. This literature compels us to grapple with the intricacies of the racialization process, how the racialization process plays out relationally, constitutively, and distinctively for particular groups. As Shu-Mei Shih puts it, the meaning of comparison is not simply "the arbitrary juxtaposition of two terms in difference and similarity" but rather, foregrounding what she describes as "submerged or displaced relationalities into view" and looking to "these relationalities as the starting point for a fuller understanding of racialization as a comparative process."[12]

A comparative race studies framework provides a useful starting point to begin to make sense of the broadening racial scope of hip-hop. Such an approach seems well suited to fully account for mutually constitutive exchanges and influences taking place among various racialized groups through their involvement in hip-hop. A number of cultural critics, for example, make the point that such an approach has the potential to yield new ways of imagining relations among groups previously viewed as having mutually exclusive histories as well as possibilities for cross-race and cross-national projects.[13] These critics look to comparative work as a means to shed light on "a neglected history of solidarity and coalition building," or what Grace Hong describes as a means to "imagine alternative modes of coalition."[14]

By the same token, a challenge is to make sense of the ways the histories of particular groups are co-implicated without ever suggesting that their positionings are identical or losing sight of the intricacies that mark relations between groups.[15] Posed another way, the danger exists given what Helen Jun has described in another context as "a teleological investment in 'interracial solidarity'—a notion that relies heavily on the premise of identification" that serves to flatten the complications that mark group relations and inter-actions.[16] A challenge in this kind of work, therefore, is to be able to account for power relations and differentials.

At the same time, *Filipinos Represent* constitutes a critical engagement with diaspora studies, building on the insight that expressive forms cannot be adequately considered by simply referencing the nation-state because it does not account for the displacements and dislocations that inflect these forms. This body of work sheds light on deterritorialized forms of identification that are very much a function and mark of the contemporary moment. My study, then, relies on a central insight of diaspora studies, the notion that such formations as identity, culture, and community cannot be contained within nation-specific rubrics or narratives. Instead, these formations defy geo-graphically bounded notions of belonging and speak to the need to account for relational networks and processes that span multiple national spaces. This insight is especially pertinent given the proliferation of hip-hop on a global scale.[17]

Moreover, my study relies on gendered accounts of the diaspora and of dias-poric youth cultural productions. This growing body of literature examines the ways in which gender and sexuality are implicated in diasporic articulations of identity, culture, and community at the same time that the diaspora serves as a space where gender and sexual norms are not simply reiterated but also reconfigured. There is particular interest in how youth diasporic cultural pro-ductions reproduce the gender ideologies of nationalist discourses, specifically the deployment and mobilization of gendered meanings and culture that posi-tion women as the embodiment of ethnic, cultural, and national boundaries. But as diaspora studies scholars point out, these cultural practices and activ-ities can also unsettle dominant articulations of gender and sexuality.[18]

I also find relevant the growing literature on the second generation. In this literature, a focus is on how this cohort relates to the parental homeland, and in particular, how members of this group express feelings of longing and belonging given their lack of firsthand experience with the homeland. Schol-ars engaged in this kind of work are especially interested in the way this cohort conceives of the parental homeland. More recent scholarship has questioned conventional constructions of the "first" and "second" genera-tions as oppositional.[19] A point of emphasis in this body of work is how the second generation turns to various expressive forms such as film and music to negotiate "culture" and "tradition" and more specifically, to create a col-lective sense identity and community that is, in many ways, distinct from that of the immigrant generation.[20]

Additionally, *Filipinos Represent* engages with an emergent Filipino cultural criticism informed by a diasporic perspective. In this kind of work, the focus is on the kinds of negotiations taking place around issues of belongingness and identity, negotiations complicated by the disjuncture between notions of home and nation. While these works do not focus on Filipino American hip-hop cultural formations, their focus on Filipino American cultural productions serves to contextualize my own work. I find especially useful their discussion of the racial implications of Filipino American cultural productions in the post–civil rights era and how culture serves as a critical terrain for elaborations of Filipino Americanness. What has yet to be adequately considered, however, is what it means for second-generation youth to claim as their own cultural forms and practices not considered traditionally their own.[21]

This study treads similar ground as a select number of recent works on hip-hop, and more specifically, Nitasha Sharma's *Hip Hop Desis: South Asian Americans, Blackness, and a Global Race Consciousness* and Anthony Kwame Harrison's *Hip-hop Underground: The Integrity and Ethics of Racial Identification.* My work is very much conversant with their works, namely our shared assumption that hip-hop constitutes a highly racialized space that is deeply enmeshed in debates about contemporary racial discourse notwithstanding deracialized accounts of hip-hop. In the case of Sharma, she looks to desi youth involvement in hip-hop as an index of the challenges and possibilities of twenty-first-century multiracial politics, especially involving South Asians and African Americans, while Harrison looks to the Bay Area hip-hop underground scene as a crucial barometer for the contours and trajectory of contemporary racial discourse. Additionally, all our works also directly engage with the producers and consumers of the culture in order to get a sense of what hip-hop means to them.[22]

Unlike these projects, however, my project aims not to uncover unanticipated points of convergence between groups previously viewed as having mutually exclusive histories or to delineate possibilities for cross-race and cross-national projects. I also do not focus on MCing, with its distinct racial dynamics and racialization history, a focal point in much of the literature in hip-hop studies. Instead, I am more interested in providing a comparative analysis of Filipino youth involvement in hip-hop (in relation to other groups of youth) and DJing (in relation to the other elements of hip-hop). As such, *Filipinos Represent* constitutes an intervention into the fields of hip-hop studies, comparative race studies, diaspora studies, and Filipino cultural criticism in terms of its comparative focus. At its broadest, it aims to open up a critical space to interrogate the continued salience of race in the evolution of hip-hop and at the same time, expand the terrain of these disciplinary formations by providing a critical engagement with the evolving dynamics of hip-hop culture.

On Methodologies: Hip-hop Literature and Filipino DJs

I employ multiple methods in this study, including an analysis of popular and academic accounts of hip-hop that delineate the cultural contexts in which hip-hop evolved and flourished. As a number of cultural critics point out, the emergence of hip-hop as a commercial and cultural force has coincided with the proliferation of journalistic and scholarly writings about hip-hop that, in turn, have become a constituent element of the cultural landscape of hip-hop. This growing body of work, however, is not merely an uninvested or disinterested study of cultural formations and social practices, just as academics and journalists are not simply documenting hip-hop history as it unfolds. Instead, hip-hop critics and writers are very much an integral part of its history, shaping its contours in the process of writing about hip-hop. As Heath puts it: "Were we to accept the idea of a fifth constitutive element of hip_hop practice, this component would arguably be the large body of cultural criticism—periodicals, fan mail, video documentaries, academic work, et cetera—by which the evolution of the culture has been and continues to be undeniably informed."[23] He goes on to make the point that "ultimately, we must maintain the presence of mind to recognize the manner in which the relationship between hip_hop culture and the critical *study* of hip-hop culture is played out in the designation of discipline and field."[24] Finally, Heath asserts that "as a discursive project, hip_hop facilitates a perpetual liminality in which and *by* which the boundaries of community and cultural history are continuously stipulated and redefined."[25]

Accordingly, I provide a discursive analysis of texts such as Steven Hagar's *Hip-hop: The Illustrated History of Break Dancing, Rap Music, and Graffiti*, David Toop's *The Rap Attack: African Jive to New York Hip-Hop*, and more recently, Harrison's *Hip-hop Underground*. The book, then, is more than a synthesis of existing analyses; it is also a reconsideration of hip-hop scholarship to draw out the ways in which knowledge of the culture is constructed, framed, and conveyed particularly around questions of origins, authenticity, and cultural belonging. This study attempts to tease out the parameters of this debate, including shifts in the prevailing discourses of hip-hop specifically as it revolves around hip-hop's perceived racial scope. It looks to journalistic and scholarly writings about hip-hop as a productive enterprise and to journalists and academics as gatekeepers of public meanings and knowledge about hip-hop. If, as Heath claims, "until lately, hip_hop studies has been, in large part, a

legitimizing project—to prove that hip_hop is worthy of institutional attention,"[26] then how has the parameters of this field of study shifted, and what
is the impetus for these shifts?

Accordingly, I provide a discursive analysis of these texts, scrutinizing how
they approach questions of race and cultural ownership. A number of questions inform my reading of these texts: How do these texts establish the parameters of hip-hop history? How is race implicated? How do these texts conceive
of the racial scope of hip-hop? On what basis and according to what terms?
How does blackness figure in early accounts of hip-hop? What kinds of shifts
have taken place in terms of the salience of blackness, and how are these
shifts tied to broader social and political transformations? In what ways does
blackness figure in contemporary hip-hop discourse?

Likewise, I also rely on personal accounts of eight Filipino DJs—four male
and four female that I interviewed for this study—in an effort to illuminate
the contours and dynamics of racialized discourses within DJ culture. These
firsthand accounts put into sharper focus those complex forms of identification taking place that simultaneously reproduce and rupture hegemonic
discourses on race and diaspora. They shed light on authenticating claims
circulating within hip-hop, specifically those revolving around questions of
cultural entitlement and authenticity. They provide a way to capture the
complexity and fluidity of racialization in everyday life in a textured and
nuanced way, and at the same time they shed light on complex social dynamics related to migration and settlement as they take place in a particular diasporic community. The aim, therefore, is not to provide a detailed picture of
the lives of Filipino DJs but rather to treat their personal narratives as cultural productions in their own right, ones that shed light on contemporary
racial and diasporic formations.

All the DJs I interviewed hail from the Bay Area, an area considered one
of the most important centers for the emergence of Filipino youth cultural
production and performance because of its high concentration of Filipino residents. It is a place where Filipino youth have been a creative force in the local
DJ scene, establishing a vibrant mobile DJ scene and playing a pivotal role in
the resurgence of DJing. The Bay Area is also home to a number of influential
Filipino DJ crews like the now disbanded Invisible Skratch Piklz (ISP) who
transformed the Bay Area into a DJ mecca and paved the way for the next
generation of Filipino DJs. The Bay Area, therefore, constitutes a vital research
site for examining the shifting boundaries of Filipinoness as they relate to U.S.
racial formations and Filipino migration and settlement.

Overview of Chapters

Chapter 1 engages critically with the contours of a burgeoning field of study that has come to be known as hip-hop studies. The chapter examines the basic narrative that circulates as "the" history of hip-hop and documents the shifting parameters of hip-hop history—what gets written as history and on what terms—through a discursive analysis of hip-hop scholarship and journalism. It traces the evolution of the perceived ethnoracial scope of hip-hop from "black" or "African American" in the 1980s to "multicultural" and "global" in the contemporary moment and explores the broader implications of this shift. More specifically, the chapter focuses on authenticity debates within hip-hop particularly as it revolves around the question of whether or not hip-hop constitutes an African American expressive form. It delineates and scrutinizes various strands of literature that have sought to complicate the construction of hip-hop as an African American expressive form.

The second chapter provides an account of the differential racialization history and trajectory of the four elements that purportedly make up hip-hop. It puts into focus how the African Americanization of hip-hop has largely been an uneven process. MCing, for example, has been the one element of hip-hop most strongly associated with blackness. In contradistinction, writing, b-boying and DJing have been historically configured as multiracial expressive forms. In the chapter, I focus in particular on the construction of DJ culture as a particular kind of (racialized) space through a discursive analysis of the kinds of racialized discourses articulated in popular accounts of DJing, including the critically acclaimed documentary *Scratch*, in which Filipino DJs play a prominent role.[27]

A profile of study participants that locates them within the context of the Filipino diaspora and delineates their level of engagement with DJ culture—what drew them to DJing, how they came up with their names, and how DJing figured in their career plans—is the focus of chapter 3. The chapter contextualizes Filipino youth involvement in DJ culture, foregrounding the significance of place and temporality—in this case the Bay Area in the 1980s—in the evolution of DJ culture. The chapter underscores how Filipino youth involvement was conditioned by developments specific to the Bay Area at a particular historical juncture.

Shedding light on the role of DJing in the formation of contemporary Filipino youth identities, chapter 4 explores how Filipino youth go about carving out a niche in an expressive form considered by many to be synonymous with blackness and the implications in terms of the negotiation of racialized meanings and identities. Based on interviews I conducted with Filipino DJs from the Bay Area, the chapter focuses on the kinds of strategies Filipino DJs rely on—*authenticating strategies* that range from efforts to foreground lived experience as the basis of their involvement in hip-hop to efforts to foreground hip-hop's transcendent appeal—strategies that are very much a function of their purported distance to blackness as well as racialization history.

Chapter 5 examines how Filipino involvement in DJing reconfigures the normative boundaries of Filipinoness predicated on nostalgia and the (re)-production of cultural linkages with an idealized homeland. As Allan Punzalan Isaac points out in *American Tropics: Articulating Filipino America*, fully accounting for Filipino social formations means coming to terms with "its 'ethnic' formation in relation to the United States, and its diasporic formation in relation to the Philippines as home."[28] In particular, chapter 5 points to the need to reconceptualize the contours of diasporic identity and culture in broader terms, in ways that take into account the kinds of complex forms of identification that diaspora opens up as well as the kinds of complications it presents *in relation* to U.S. racial formations.

But while DJing has enabled Filipino youth to broaden the bounds of Filipinoness, it serves to reinforce heteronormative notions of Filipinoness. In this chapter, I scrutinize how DJ culture constitutes a highly gendered and stratified space through which Filipino youth can adopt, generate, and redefine conventional gender and heterosexual norms, including established meanings of masculinity and femininity in complex and contradictory ways. DJing may very well serve as a site of cultural affirmation for various groups of youth, including Filipino youth, but when it comes to issues of gender and sexuality, it is a mainly conservative arena. Nonetheless, this has not precluded female DJs from carving out a niche and fashioning themselves on their own terms.

In the interest of pursuing a broader critique of culture, the conclusion explores the wider implications of the theoretical and substantive issues raised throughout the book. The chapter reiterates the broader stakes of the project via a consideration of the trope of nation, a trope that enjoys a great deal of currency within hip-hop. I am interested in how nationness is imagined within the context of hip-hop and, in particular, how the borders of the hip-hop nation have become a point of contention among hip-hop practitioners—who belongs, who does not, and on what basis. I argue that the trope of nation and its attendant controversies is symptomatic of the paucity of a critical vocabulary around issues of cultural engagement, difference, and race in the post–civil rights era. Relying on an emergent Filipino American cultural criticism, I consider DJing in relation to other Filipino American expressive forms and how nation is implicated in these forms. I end this chapter with a discussion of the broader implications for the ways in which we theorize the dynamics of culture, the intricacies of race, and the workings of power in the contemporary moment.

Chapter 1 The African Americanization of Hip-hop

> Even during its humble beginnings hip-hop was never strictly a
> black thing. It has always been multiracial, multicultural, and
> multilingual. Those qualities formed a movement that has defied
> all attempts to impose the strict racial definitions and caricatures
> that endeavor to limit its potential reach and influence. By insisting
> on borrowing from various cultural, musical, aesthetic, and political
> traditions, hip-hop became an incredibly rich fountainhead of youth
> creativity and expression. While black youth play a central role in
> hip-hop, white Latino, and Asian youths continue to make their
> mark on the movement, too.
>
> —S. Craig Watkins, *Hip-hop Matters: Politics, Pop Culture, and
> the Struggle for the Soul of the Movement*

IN RECENT YEARS, scholarly and popular discourse addressing hip-hop
and its various articulations has grown exponentially to the point where
there is now a fairly substantial body of work that can be categorized under
the rubric of "hip-hop studies." The growth of this literature, however, has
not proven to be seamless. Instead, it has come to be characterized by contentious debates and discussions revolving around a particular set of issues,
what I consider fault lines within the literature. As hip-hop has emerged as a
cultural force on a global scale, it has come under critical scrutiny not just
among those at the periphery of the culture but also among those who consider themselves core members. There has been a good deal of debate and
discussion, for example, regarding the commercialization of hip-hop on a
global scale and its impact on the culture's dynamism, politics, and integrity,
prompting declarations of hip-hop's demise.[1] There has also been a good deal
of debate and discussion regarding the gender and sexual politics of hip-hop,
and in particular, the pervasiveness of sexism, misogyny, and homophobia in
the culture.[2]

1

No single issue, however, has generated more heated debate and discussion than the issue of cultural origins, entitlement, and authenticity, particularly as it revolves around hip-hop's apparent "blackness." As Anthony Kwame Harrison puts it, "hip-hop, more so than any other musical style, has been mired in deliberations over authenticity."[3] Inez H. Templeton characterizes the debate this way: "The question of whether or not race is (or should be) a factor in hip-hop practices, as well as the consideration of the authentic within the context of hip-hop's global consumption, have generated polarizing debates among hip-hop fans as well as scholars, making it difficult to uncover balanced analyses of these issues."[4] Hip-hop's apparent blackness, in other words, has come under a great deal of critical scrutiny and generated highly divergent perspectives.

The epigraph that opens this chapter signifies the "multiracial, multicultural, and multilingual" turn in hip-hop historiography,[5] the notion that from the outset, hip-hop constituted an expressive form subject to multiple influences and traditions obscured by its construction as an African American form of expression. But as evidenced by the following quote from Bakari Kitwana, this kind of claim has not gone uncontested even as cultural critics like Kitwana acknowledge the multiple origins and influences of hip-hop: "Yes, it's become en vogue to imagine hip-hop as belonging to everyone. Sure, there have been other cultural influences. But influences are just that, influences. Black American cultural attitudes, style, verbal and body language, as well as insider Black cultural perspective, not only were prevalent at hip-hop's origin but remain at its core today."[6] The two quotes are symptomatic of the kinds of exchanges that have occurred and the terms by which they have taken place. The debate hinges on whether or not hip-hop constitutes an African American expressive form but also the extent to which hip-hop signifies blackness even as it has evolved into a global expressive form.

While at one point hip-hop was seen as unquestionably an African American expressive form, that is no longer the case. Instead, the emphasis in much contemporary literature has been on hip-hop's complex genealogies and trajectories that exceed the bounds of blackness. An emergent theme is that it can no longer be assumed that hip-hop is an exclusively African American terrain, although it remains strongly marked as the domain of African Americans. No longer are African American youth considered the sole or primary innovators of the culture. Thus, the kind of "insider" status historically accorded African American youth has been cast into doubt given the expansion of the perceived racial scope of hip-hop. Also coming under critical scrutiny are notions of authenticity predicated on signifiers of blackness. According to much contemporary literature, to speak of hip-hop in terms of blackness is to engage in essentialism and to subscribe to reductive notions of race and culture. This points to the tenuous status of blackness within hip-hop as well as conventional narratives of hip-hop that hitherto placed African Americans at the center of its foundational narrative.

In this chapter, I provide a critical consideration of early hip-hop literature and the ways this body of work has served to establish the parameters of what is generally considered the foundational narrative of hip-hop history and culture, including its purported African Americanness. However, I am not so much concerned with evaluating the historical fidelity of these accounts as I am with the broader implications for claims of cultural origins, entitlement, and legitimacy. Thus, I consider several strands of literature that have sought to complicate the racial grounds on which to consider the genealogy and various articulations of hip-hop. While acknowledging hip-hop's black antecedents, these works call for a more nuanced narration of hip-hop history, one that does not underplay or underestimate the varied origins and influences of hip-hop. Accordingly, these writings lay out compelling arguments for broadening our understanding of the contours of hip-hop history and culture.

In one strand of this literature, a focal point is a reconsideration of the seminal role that Puerto Rican and West Indian youth played in development of hip-hop, while another strand focuses on the Afro-diasporic origins and influences of hip-hop, the notion that from the very beginning hip-hop constituted a transnational expressive form. In yet another strand, a focal point is the diffusion of hip-hop on a global scale and what it means for hip-hop to be taken up in contexts far removed from its South Bronx origins. In the conclusion of this chapter, I then examine the broader theoretical and political implications raised by this literature in terms of the ways we think about the intricacies of race and the dynamics of culture through a consideration of more recent literature that directly grapples with questions of race, authenticity, and difference.

Early Accounts of Hip-hop

Early historical accounts of hip-hop continue to have a great deal of currency and resonance, establishing the parameters of what is generally considered the master or foundational narrative of the culture. Steven Hager's *Hip-hop: The Illustrated History of Break Dancing, Rap Music, and Graffiti*, published in 1984, is in many ways illustrative of the ways the initial wave of hip-hop literature set (and continues to do so) the bounds of hip-hop historiography.

Still referenced by much contemporary literature, it traces the emergence of hip-hop and articulates a narrative that revolves around a set of themes and tropes—for example, the notion that the emergence of hip-hop was a testament to the resiliency and creativity of marginalized youth, hip-hop as providing a viable alternative to gangs, and style and competition as defining features of the culture—that are recapitulated and reaffirmed in contemporary accounts of hip-hop, to the extent that they now seem transparent and self-evident.[7]

The notion of the South Bronx as the birthplace of hip-hop has become a foundational theme of hip-hop historiography, and like other foundational themes of the literature, it is repeatedly and constantly invoked in both popular and scholarly accounts. Hager's book begins with a consideration of the South Bronx, serving to cement the neighborhood's mythic status in the foundational narrative of hip-hop. In chapter 1 (entitled "The Bronx on Fire"), Hager documents the dramatic decline of the Bronx, its transformation from a fairly stable middle-class neighborhood to a place wracked by devastation that would pave the way for the mass exodus of Bronx residents and ultimately, the rise of expressive forms that have come to be associated with hip-hop.

Additionally, Hager subscribes to what Owen J. Dwyer has described in another context as the theory of the "'Great Man' of history,"[8] privileging the contributions of a select number of individuals over the involvement of countless numbers of youth in the emergence and evolution of hip-hop. More specifically, the book foregrounds the innovations of the so-called "holy trinity" of hip-hop—Kool Herc, Afrika Bambaataa, and Grandmaster Flash—who typically have their own chapters documenting their exploits. In this kind of formulation, hip-hop is represented as a by-product and function of the greatness of a select cadre of (male) individuals.

Hager's book also subscribes to the notion of hip-hop as comprising various expressive forms, and dedicates separate chapters on writing and b-boying and reinforcing what has become yet another foundation theme of hip-hop literature and writing. He references a *Village Voice* article by Richard Goldstein published in December 1980, which he considers significant because of the way "it linked graffiti and rap music for the first time."[9] He then goes on to cite Goldstein: "In fact, the graffiti sensibility has a musical equivalent in 'rap records'—another rigid, indecipherable form that can sustain great complexity."[10] Hager proceeds to voice his assent with Goldstein's contention: "Although Goldstein's awareness of rap music was probably limited (most of his readers undoubtedly didn't even know what the term meant), his assumption that rap sprang from the same cultural conditions as graffiti was correct."[11] Relations among the different elements, however, are often assumed rather than demonstrated. In the case of Hager, he postulates a symbiotic relationship among the various expressive forms: "The commercial success of rap music furthered graffiti. Mention of the writers began appearing in the music press, and several prominent writers went on to record rap records, including Phase 2, Futura, and Brathwaite."[12]

Another theme reinscribed in early hip-hop literature is the notion of hip-hop as an expressive form rooted in African American cultural practices and traditions. Hager, for example, makes the following point: "Although it is difficult to trace the origins of rap, the genre is firmly embedded in black American culture and stretches farther than even most rappers realize."[13] In *The Rap Attack: African Jive to New York Hip-Hop*, David Toop makes a similar point: "No matter how far Bambaataa and others like him may go in their outlandish selections of source material or their desire for internationalism, the music always returns to two basis elements—a funky drumbeat and some spoken or chanted words. Both spring from an abundant Afro-American tradition."[14] In the case of MCing, Toop traces its genealogy squarely within African American cultural practices and traditions: "If the hip-hop message and protest rappers had ancestry in the savannah griots, the Bronx braggers, boasters and verbal abusers are children of the black American word games known as signifying and the dozens."[15]

In another early hip-hop text, entitled *Fresh: Hip-hop Don't Stop*, published in 1985, Nelson George similarly conceives of rap as an African American expressive form: "Part of any rapper's appeal is pure charisma; he is confident, even cocky, and his stories reveal his strong sense of the world and his place in it. To that degree, a good rapper is firmly in the tradition of those proud Afro-American egotists Muddy Waters, Bo Diddley, James Brown, even heavyweight champ Muhammad Ali."[16] Indeed, George continues in this mode: "Will rap last? Just like doo-wop, blues, jazz, soul, and all the musical idioms of Afro-Americans, rap speaks to both the race that created it and the people of all backgrounds that it fascinates."[17]

This is not to suggest that in these early accounts, there was no acknowledgment of the varied origins and influences of hip-hop. David Toop delineates the links between the Caribbean and New York:

> Although reggae was relatively unknown to most black Americans in the early '70s the links between New York and the Caribbean are strong. In the 1930s almost one-quarter of Harlem's residents were from the West Indies. For Grandmaster Flash, whose parents came from Barbados (his father collected

records of both Caribbean music and American swing), it was the "monstrous" sound system of Kool DJ Herc which dominated hip-hop in its formative days. Herc came from Kingston, Jamaica, in 1967, when the toasting or DJ style of his own country was still fairly new. Giant speaker boxes were essential in the competitive world of Jamaican sound systems (sound-system battles were and still are central to the reggae scene) and Herc murdered the Bronx opposition with his volume and shattering frequency range.[18]

What is significant about the foregoing is that, in order to establish the Afro-Caribbean influences of hip-hop, it has become a standard move in hip-hop historiography to reference Herc and, in particular, his immersion in Jamaican sound system culture as a child before he migrated to the United States in 1967.

Along the same lines, Hager goes over the role of Puerto Rican youth in the evolution of b-boying in his historical account of hip-hop. He emphasizes how some of the most prominent b-boy crews such as the Rock Steady Crew comprised largely Puerto Rican youth. Hager recounts how Puerto Ricans got into breaking during the time that African American youth seemingly lost interest in the art and in the process of doing so, provided the impetus for the evolution of b-boy culture.[19] Nonetheless, for both Hager and Toop, hip-hop constitutes an undeniably African American expressive form. Accordingly, these early accounts would help establish the basis for the close association between hip-hop and African Americanness.

More recently, however, cultural critics have reconsidered, complicated, and questioned what previously have been considered fundamental tenets of hip-hop historiography. To illustrate, the South Bronx may be hip-hop's birthplace, but it is no longer assumed that youth in surrounding areas did not engage in similar practices or that the different expressive forms constitutive of hip-hop just suddenly came together in the South Bronx, what one writer has aptly called the "romanticized Big Bang theory" of hip-hop.[20] As Raquel Z. Rivera notes, "the creative impulses behind hip-hop and the actual practices themselves were not exclusive to the South Bronx. Young people in other city neighborhoods participated in expressive phenomena related to what eventually became known as hip-hop culture, at times unaware that these expressions were not confined to the borders of their immediate community."[21] Joseph G. Schloss makes a similar point when it comes to the diverse origins and histories of b-boying, the need to not only consider other locales as Brooklyn but also the historiographical implications of such a move.[22] The standard narrative of hip-hop, in other words, may very well overprivilege the South Bronx obscuring the role of other places and locales in the evolution of hip-hop. The one proposition that has come under the most intense scrutiny, however, is the notion of hip-hop as an African American expressive form with criticisms emanating from multiple vantage points and multiple strands of literature.

The Puerto Rican and Afro-Caribbean Presence in the Evolution of Hip-hop

One strand of literature aims to establish the formative role of Puerto Rican youth in the emergence and evolution of hip-hop, making a compelling case that hip-hop needs to be seen within a broader cultural framework that can illuminate the "creative coauthorship"[23] of hip-hop and accommodate the shared history and cultural heritage between Puerto Ricans and African Americans. Alongside black youth (as well as West Indian youth), Puerto Rican youth were there from the very beginning, making their mark as co-creators and innovators in all the constituent elements of hip-hop, including rap, years before hip-hop became a mass commercial form. In Juan Flores's words: "Without denying the catalytic and enduring presence of West Indians in Harlem and other African American communities or the likely interplay between rhythm and blues and reggae traditions, it is Puerto Ricans who most directly shared with young African Americans the demographic base and creative stage of hip-hop in its origins."[24] For Flores, hip-hop constitutes yet another moment in the long history of black–Puerto Rican mutual collaborations and exchanges. Accordingly, the emergence and subsequent evolution of hip-hop only makes sense within the broader context of shared black and Puerto Rican cultural traditions and practices.

Flores, however, makes the point that popular understandings of hip-hop have served to elide the role of Puerto Rican youth as core participants in the evolution of hip-hop. Instead, "rap is either particularized as a 'black thing,' generalized as a multicultural 'youth thing,' or variegated into a set of sub-categories ('gangsta rap,' 'message rap,' 'female rap,' and so on) which in the last few years has come to include 'Latino rap.'"[25] Flores proceeds to make the point that these standard formulations of rap are problematic because of their failure to account for the specificities of the relationship of Puerto Ricans to hip-hop. More specifically, these formulations elide the conjunction between Puerto Rican and African American cultural traditions and practices that paved the way for the emergence of hip-hop.

Building on and extending Flores's analysis, Rivera likewise challenges the African Americanization of hip-hop and foregrounds the centrality of Puerto Rican youth to hip-hop's formative moments. She takes issue, in particular, with accounts that view Puerto Ricanness and African Americanness as mutually exclusive categories. Instead, Rivera makes the point that Puerto Ricans need to be seen as part of the African diaspora in the Americas:

> Puerto Ricans in the United States are commonly thought of as being part of this country's Hispanic or Latino population. But Puerto Ricans are also considered an exception among Latinos. Their exceptionality is based on a history that diverges from what has been construed as the Latino norm and that bears much in common with the experience of African Americans. Furthermore, Puerto Ricans share common ground with African Americans not only because of their similar socioeconomic experiences as racialized ethnic minorities in the United States but also because Puerto Rican culture is as Spanish as it is African, thus making it part of the myriad group experiences that make up the African diaspora in the Americas.[26]

For Rivera, then, hip-hop constitutes an important realm of cultural collaboration between Puerto Ricans and African Americans, what she describes as "a cultural zone of intense interaction and cooperation" rather than the exclusive property of African Americans.[27]

Like Flores, Rivera focuses on how Puerto Rican youth involvement in hip-hop cannot be accommodated within standard conceptions of blackness and Puerto Ricanness precisely because conventional understandings of these formations are predicated on a static view of culture and identity. Blackness, for example, tends to be understood solely through the experiences of African Americans, while Puerto Ricanness tends to be understood in what she describes as "Hispanocentric and island-bound" terms.[28] In either case, Puerto Rican involvement in hip-hop is seen as incompatible with both blackness (i.e., an intrusion into a black realm) and Puerto Ricanness (i.e., a betrayal of culture).

On the Afro-Diasporic Origins and Influences of Hip-hop

Another strand of literature aims to challenge the African Americanization of hip-hop from a diasporic perspective. Paul Gilroy's *The Black Atlantic: Modernity and Double Consciousness* has proven to be a highly influential work delineating the limitations of relying on the frame of nation as a unit of analysis of cultural and political formations. Gilroy takes issue with the nationalist focus in both British and U.S.-based cultural studies that renders cultural expressions coextensive with national borders, what he describes as the "the fatal junction of the concept of nationality with the concept of culture."[29] For Gilroy, black cultural politics and formations cannot be adequately considered by simply referencing the internal dynamics of any one nation. Instead, a transnational and intercultural framework is required to begin to account for the intricacies of black history, which encompasses a network of cultural exchanges and transformations spanning Africa, the Caribbean, the United States, and Europe. In the case of hip-hop, its history cannot be framed within the confines of a nation and its borders.[30]

From this vantage point, Gilroy challenges the racialization of hip-hop as an exclusively African American phenomenon, as well as the notion that hip-hop is the absolute ethnic property of African Americans. Conceptualizing hip-hop this way, he argues, effectively erases its origins in the black diaspora and the formative role of black diasporic cultural practices in its emergence. Notwithstanding its multiple origins and influences, however, considerations of hip-hop continue to be informed by African American exceptionalism, as evidenced by the use of the term "rap" or the deployment of accounts that conceive of hip-hop as a direct descendant of jazz, soul, and the blues, all of which Gilroy argues are more evocative of African American influences and genealogies. Instead, he calls for an alternative understanding of hip-hop and other black cultural productions that is not rooted in discourses of nationalism and ethnic exceptionalism but one that is predicated on a recognition of the syncretic character of black cultural formations.[31]

Gilroy also takes issue with how music has become an important medium to make authenticating claims and, in the case of hip-hop, a potent signifier of racial authenticity and blackness in particular. He finds especially troubling the valorization of African American–based hip-hop by African American scholars as authentic and the concomitant devaluation of hip-hop rooted in other locations in the black diaspora as inauthentic, a function of its purported distance from a specific (and identifiable) point of origin. What potentially can serve as a vehicle for unsettling the notion of authenticity (because of its syncretic character), therefore, has been deployed as signifier of authenticity. Gilroy goes on to assert that the issue of authenticity has not only persisted but assumed greater significance among practitioners, consumers, and fans alike even with the proliferation of hip-hop-related styles and genres on a global scale. Authenticity has actually enhanced the appeal of black cultural forms and has become an integral part of the ways these forms are marketed, packaged, and sold.[32]

On Hip-hop, Blackness, and the Global Diffusion of Hip-hop

In the wake of the diffusion of hip-hop throughout the world, a body of writing has emerged that maps out global articulations of hip-hop and its diversity. It looks into the ways hip-hop is constantly made and remade in specific locations as well as the ways the global diffusion of hip-hop has given rise to new cultural forms and identities. For cultural critics engaged in this kind of work, hip-hop's emergence as a global phenomenon provides a comparative context for thinking through hip-hop's articulations in the United States as compared to other places. For these critics, it does not make sense to view hip-hop as a U.S.-based expressive form exported to different parts of the globe because of the way it has been adapted to local circumstances for local purposes. A focal point in this scholarship is what it means for hip-hop to be diffused throughout the world and taken up in settings and contexts far removed from its South Bronx origins. These works are particularly concerned with how youth across the globe with little historical connection to the creators and originators of the culture go about carving out a niche and legitimizing their place within hip-hop.[33]

Coming under critical scrutiny in this body of writing is not only the notion of hip-hop as an African American phenomenon but also as a nation-based phenomenon. In the introduction to *Global Noise: Rap and Hip-hop outside the U.S.A.*, for example, editor Tony Mitchell asserts that the roots of hip-hop are not simply African American but "culturally, eclectically, and syncretically wide-ranging as they are deep."[34] Given the varied origins and extensive influences of hip-hop, therefore, it would be more appropriate to argue "for the locality, temporality, and 'universality' of hip-hop."[35] Mitchell goes on to make the point that "Hip-hop and rap cannot be viewed simply as an expression of African American culture; it has become a vehicle for global youth affiliations and a tool for reworking local identity all over the world."[36]

In the process of analyzing burgeoning hip-hop scenes outside the United States, a number of the contributors to *Global Noise* decenter the United States as the focal point of hip-hop production and innovation and expand the grounds from which to consider notions of "origins," "roots," and "authenticity." Accordingly, there has been a shift in focus from deciphering origins to accounting for the multifaceted articulations of hip-hop in different parts of the globe, particularly among those "who may share no historical relationship with blacks but who find in hip-hop a language, a set of resources, and knowledge with which to articulate similar but not identical struggles and concerns."[37]

For cultural critic Robin D. G. Kelley it is not simply the case that hip-hop has gone global. In many ways, it has always been global from its inception. One only has to look at the diasporic backgrounds of its creators and innovators: "Contrary to recent media claims, hip-hop hasn't 'gone global.' It has been global, or international at least, since its birth in the very local neighborhoods of the South Bronx, Washington Heights, and Harlem. While the music, break-dancing, and graffiti writing that make up the components of hip-hop culture are often associated with African American urban youth, hip-hop's inventors also included the sons and daughters of immigrants who had been displaced by the movement of global capital."[38] Kelley goes on to make the point that hip-hop's global character is not incidental to but constitutive of hip-hop's development, which is rooted in displacements brought about by the forces of globalization. The genealogy and trajectory of hip-hop, in other words, only makes sense within a global or transnational frame.

Hip-hop as an African American Expressive Form

While critiques of hip-hop as primarily an African American form have gained currency, there are those who continue to subscribe to that notion. Cultural critic Imani Perry directly engages with Gilroy's work, positing that the notion of hip-hop as a black cultural formation is not necessarily incompatible with the notion of hip-hop as multiracial. She poses the following question to accentuate her point: "Why can't something be black (read, *black* American) and be influenced by a number of cultures and styles at the same time?"[39]

Perry takes issue with diasporic critiques of hip-hop, particularly Paul Gilroy's use of the black Atlantic as his unit of analysis for making sense of the historical origins and trajectory of hip-hop. For Perry, such a framework fails to do justice to "the manner in which the music became integrated into the fabric of American culture, [which] was as a black American cultural product, through an overwhelmingly black American audience (no longer the case), and using black American aesthetics as signature features of the music."[40] In her view, Gilroy's use of a transnational framework presumes a kind of unity among blacks of the African diaspora that ultimately serves to obscure the specificities of the African American experience. Instead, Perry subscribes to the notion that in order to fully account for the trajectory of hip-hop, one has to consider it within a national frame.

For Perry, then, hip-hop is very much a direct extension of African American oral, music, and protest traditions. She makes the point that hip-hop's use of boasting and signifying is very much rooted in African American cultural practices and traditions. Perry also makes the point that just because hip-hop has been subject to multiple influences, it does not mean that it cannot also be black. African American expressive forms, in other words, have never been pure or monolithic but have always been influenced by and have incorporated different cultures and styles.[41] As Robin D. G. Kelley puts it in another context, "to say it is a 'black' thing does not mean it is made up entirely of black things."[42] Black expressive forms have never been pure or monolithic but characterized by hybridity.

John Szwed subscribes to a similar point of view, asserting that notwithstanding its multiple origins and influences, hip-hop constitutes an undeniably African American form. For Szwed, hip-hop, like anything else that originates in the United States, is "creole": "But having noted rap's broad affinities, its American-ness, its creole emergence, and its lack of exclusive rights to be offensive, no one would be fooled into missing the fact that it finally is also very much an African-American form."[43] Cultural critic Bakari Kitwana echoes Szwed's point: "To begin with, it must be stated unequivocally that hip-hop is a subculture of Black American youth culture—period."[44] Like Szwed, Kitwana recognizes the multiple influences of hip-hop, but in his view this does not detract from hip-hop's African American core as evidenced by his remark earlier in this chapter. For Kitwana, then, notions of hip-hop as an African American expressive form and an expressive form subject to multiple influences are not mutually exclusive.[45]

Even cultural critics who subscribe to the perspective that hip-hop constitutes a global form of expression have voiced reservations about the broader implications of this kind of perspective. While the emergence of hip-hop as the lingua franca of youth across the globe has rendered problematic the conception of hip-hop as a "black thing," cultural critics acknowledge that race remains a crucial component of hip-hop, what Ian Condry describes as the "complicated racial matrix at the heart of hip-hop's worldwide diffusion."[46]

There is the concern among some cultural critics that an affirmation of hip-hop's transnational dimensions can obscure its "rootedness" in American culture and in particular, African American culture. The editors of as well as a number of the contributors to the anthology *The Vinyl Ain't Final*, for example, are quick to point out that foregrounding hip-hop's "transnational" roots should not be taken as an uncritical celebration of hip-hop's hybridity or a disavowal of black roots. The editors make the point that notwithstanding its transnational dimensions, blackness continues to be a focal point in hip-hop formations worldwide. They argue that this is not simply a matter or a question of "Americocentrism." Rather, it is symptomatic of the ways the United States continues to serve as the center of hip-hop production and dissemination as well as the ways blackness resonates among youth across the globe.[47]

In "Global Black Self-Fashionings: Hip-hop as Diasporic Space," Marc D. Perry makes the point that "although hip-hop has undergone radical transformation from street to international marketplace, it has retained a critical capacity to convey a signifying blackness of aesthetic form and emotive force."[48] He goes on to make the point that "when considering the international proliferation of hip-hop one needs to be cognizant of the differing ways hip-hop's black signified cultural politics travel as they are engaged by communities beyond their initial sites of U.S. production."[49] While Perry agrees with someone like Tony Mitchell, who asserts that hip-hop cannot be viewed as synonymous with African Americanness, he raises the issue of how blackness continues to frame the reception of hip-hop worldwide.

Contemporary Scholarship and the Question of Race

More recent works continue to grapple with issues of race, authenticity, and genealogy in relation to hip-hop. A select number of these works directly engage with the foregoing debates and discussions, foregrounding the prominence of race in shaping the dynamics and discourses of hip-hop. I want to focus in particular on Nitasha Tamar Sharma's *Hip-hop Desis* and Anthony Kwame Harrison's *Hip-hop Underground* because their engagement with race speaks to the complexities and challenges of making sense of contemporary racial politics through a consideration of hip-hop. Like my own work, these works operate from the assumption that hip-hop constitutes a highly racialized terrain utilized by various groups of youth to negotiate racial meanings and categories.

In *Hip-hop Desis*, Sharma investigates the nature of desi identification with blackness and in particular, how desi artists turn to hip-hop to negotiate with their racial status and create a sense of what it means to be desi. Sharma is particularly interested in the ways her respondents contend with accepted notions of race and the ways they articulate their own meanings of race. In doing so, desi artists revise the contours of both desiness and blackness as well as Americanness and hip-hop culture, exhibiting what she terms as a "global race consciousness" in which race constitutes "a matter of critical understanding—of ways of thinking about and being in the world rather than a reference to an individual's biology or phenotype."[50]

Desi artists subscribe to the notion of hip-hop as an African American expressive form but nonetheless attempt to define their place within it. For some of Sharma's interviewees, hip-hop does not necessarily and inevitably function as space to transcend difference, but rather a space to work through difference. According to Sharma, desi artists do not evade questions of race or difference but instead deal with these issues head-on. South Asians also look to hip-hop as a vehicle for the creation of identifications between South Asians and African Americans. Desi artists take an active part in the production of race that could then serve as a basis for cross-racial identifications.

Rather than a site of deracination, then, Sharma looks to hip-hop as a potential site for race-based identifications that shed light on the complexities of intergroup dynamics.

In terms of her own perspective, Sharma acknowledges the multiracial and global nature of hip-hop, yet she also makes the point that this should not be taken to mean that hip-hop in some way has transcended race. In her view, "hip-hop is not *either* a multiracial art form *or* a black one. Rather, it is a multiracial production of black popular culture."[51] She goes on to pose the question of "how much more productive would it be if we were to reorient the ownership/authenticity debate by focusing on an artist's *approach* to hip-hop, rather than on an artist's identity? This anti-essentialist approach evaluates the artists' motives, skills, and locations within urban culture without erasing hip-hop as an American Black cultural formation deeply attendant to the politics of race that also extends beyond those commonly considered 'Black.'"[52] Ultimately, Sharma finds the terms of the existing debate lacking and favors a third perspective, what one of her respondents characterizes as "wider black consciousness."[53] She subscribes to the notion of hip-hop as a black expressive form but "black" in terms of consciousness or political ideology. For Sharma, this kind of perspective is valuable because of the way it compels us to reassess and come to terms with the shifting parameters of blackness without eliding its continued relevance.

Sharma's *Hip-hop Desis* is part of a burgeoning literature on Afro-Asian interconnections that aims to render intelligible the mutual cultural imbrications and influences between the two groups that are not assimilable to conventional narratives of Asian American history or to African American history. She views South Asian involvement in hip-hop as another moment in a long history of Afro-Asian cultural exchanges, one that is illustrative of the mutually constitutive relations between the two groups. While this body of work is useful in terms of illuminating the ways Asian American youth go about negotiating the racialization of hip-hop as African American given the absence of historical, cultural, and class continuities between the originators of hip-hop and themselves, it is limited in terms of illuminating Filipino American hip-hop formations. More to the point, the specificities of Filipino youth involvement in hip-hop are not easily mapped onto the rubric or frame that scholars engaged in this kind of work deploy.

In contrast, Harrison focuses on the Bay Area hip-hop underground sphere and how members of this scene grapple with issues of race and difference in a hip-hop scene that has come to be known for its diversity. His book sheds light on how race in the United States will be imagined and performed in the new millennium: "Some of the most compelling dialogues on race in American popular culture take place within underground hip-hop, where largely middle-class, multiracial constituencies of young people navigate a transforming racial landscape."[54] For Harrison, then, the underground serves as a crucial barometer for the kinds of dialogues revolving around race and anticipates the contours of racial discourse on a national scale.

In opposition to the mainstream rap scene, the hip-hop underground scene is not wholly dependent on conventional notions of blackness. Instead, it operates according to a different racial logic than commercial rap music. Given its demographic makeup, the scene provides an alternative notion of hip-hop authenticity and legitimacy. Harrison is especially interested in how this scene has opened up new lines of identification not wedded to blackness. In short, ethnic and racial identifications are not paramount in this scene, at least on the surface.

Harrison asserts, however, that despite its avowed color blindness, race insinuates itself in a multitude of ways in this scene. For white MCs, their involvement in hip-hop serves as a vehicle to confound normative notions of whiteness, while for Filipino artists, it serves as a vehicle to explore linkages with other historically marginalized groups that could potentially form the basis for multiracial and multiethnic partnerships. Ultimately, Harrison concludes: "Here I peremptorily reject any notion of color-blindness, instead insisting that the opportunity for hip-hoppers of all shades and colors to legitimately participate does not occur on equal terms."[55]

Conclusion

The "multiracial, multicultural, and multilingual" in hip-hop historiography has served well to broaden the bounds of hip-hop historiography.[56] Providing a corrective to what cultural critics perceive as African American–centered accounts, this body of work has reconfigured the terms by which hip-hop has been understood, and in the process, opened up alternative modes of validating authenticity. This turn in the literature, however, has also raised questions and complications that it has yet to adequately theorize. To illustrate, scholarship has left underexplored what is at stake when blackness is invoked either as a way to claim or problematize claims of cultural ownership (typically through charges of essentialism). The differences and contradictions among various groups of youth have also been underexplored, and thus there is a risk of divesting groups of their specificity.

But it is not just the formative role and involvement of non–African American youth and its global diffusion that has troubled claims of hip-hop as an

African American phenomenon. Also complicating this claim is the attention given to the distinctive racialization history and trajectory of the four elements that purportedly make up hip-hop. This has put into focus not only how the African Americanization of hip-hop has largely been an uneven process but also how issues of cultural belonging and entitlement have played out differently among the various elements of hip-hop.

Chapter 2 The Racialization of DJ Culture

> When people say that "Hip-hop is a black thing, or a Puerto Rican thing," I feel like saying, "You know what? Let me explain something to you, because you weren't there." It takes a lot of nerve to say that. Our art is multiracial, multicultural, multilingual, multidimensional . . . So when people tell me that hip-hop is a black thing, I'm like "Where? Where? That's a lie." Most of the writers I knew were Hispanic, black, Asian, and white.
>
> —CRASH, *Aerosol Kingdom: Subway Painters of New York City*, 2002

IN THE ONGOING DEBATE over the racial scope and boundaries of hip-hop it has been underspecified how the African Americanization of hip-hop has largely been an uneven process with particular elements (i.e., MCing and DJing) more closely aligned to blackness at particular historical moments, while other elements (such as writing and breaking) are perceived in more "inclusive" terms—that is, as forms that cut across ethnic, racial, and class lines. Media representations of b-boying and writing, for instance, configured these expressive forms in terms more of class than race.[1] This would have implications in terms of how particular groups go about claiming legitimacy and, by the same token, how the issue of cultural entitlement would play out for each constituent element of hip-hop. The issue of cultural entitlement, in other words, varied for the diverse aspects of hip-hop.

Accordingly, cultural critics have begun to map out the differential racialization history and trajectory of each constituent element of hip-hop, or at least take notice of them. Like the literature considered in chapter 1, this literature aims to complicate the genealogy and foundational narrative of hip-hop predicated on its racialization as African American. And particularly relevant for this study, critics have also begun to scrutinize how issues of cultural belonging and entitlement have played out in overlapping but also divergent ways among what are considered the constituent elements of hip-hop. Organic relations among these different elements, in other words, can no longer be assumed. This is not to suggest that parallels do not exist among the various elements but rather to suggest that these links cannot be taken for granted.

Coming under critical scrutiny are not only the ways practitioners of the various elements view their respective subculture, but also how the media, commodity culture, and the prevailing racial logic of the United States are all implicated in the racialization process and, in particular, the differential racialization of the constituent elements of hip-hop.[2] Additionally, the focus on the differential racialization of hip-hop has served to trouble accounts that view and approach hip-hop as a monolithic expressive form. What emerges are elaborate and contested historical accounts that serve to further complicate hip-hop's genealogy and trajectory predicated on a one-to-one correspondence between hip-hop and blackness.

Beginning with a consideration of MCing, this chapter examines the construction of each constituent element of hip-hop as a particular kind of racialized space with implications for claims of cultural belonging and entitlement. It explores recurrent themes in the respective literature focusing on a particular element of hip-hop. The chapter addresses the question of why particular elements are more aligned with blackness than other elements and explores how this process is very much contested, subject to competing claims and visions. It foregrounds the vexed relations among the constitutive elements of hip-hop hitherto obscured by standard accounts of hip-hop.

MCing as an Extension of African American Oral Practices and Traditions

Notwithstanding acknowledgment of the formative role of Afro-Caribbean youth in the evolution of hip-hop and the convergence between Afro-Caribbean and African American cultural histories, prevailing accounts of hip-hop have until recently constructed it as, in Rivera's words, "lodged within an exclusively African American matrix,"[3] particularly in the case of MCing and DJing. Rivera also notes, however, that the African Americanization of hip-hop or, more to the point, the link between blackness and hip-hop has not always been clear, straightforward, and unambiguous. Rather, it is a function of the convergence of multiple social forces including the mass commodification of rap and the widespread perception that MCing and DJing are rooted in African American oral and musical traditions that has set the stage for the African Americanization of hip-hop and, in particular, of rap and DJing.

A key moment in Rivera's discussion is the mid-1980s, a period marked by the commercial ascendancy of rap and the concomitant commercial decline of DJing, breaking, and writing that has come to inform popular understandings of hip-hop. The mass commodification of rap and its subsequent entry into the mainstream, however, not only meant the conflation of hip-hop with rap but also the intensification of the association between blackness and MCing. Rivera contends that the mass commodification of rap was predicated on a narrow notion of blackness, the kind of logic that presumed a one-to-one correspondence between cultural boundaries and racial boundaries.

Rivera also points the finger at the prevailing racial logic of the United States predicated on the discreteness of racial categories and more specifically, reductive notions of culture and identity that has come to inform popular understandings of hip-hop. Given its varied origins and influences, hip-hop does not neatly fit in prevailing U.S. racial categories and yet, precisely because of the extant racial logic, it is considered in either-or terms and slotted as belonging to a singular racial category. It becomes very difficult, therefore, to fully account for the complicated genealogy of an expressive form such as hip-hop.

Another contributing factor is the perceived linguistic and musical core of hip-hop that has rendered it as susceptible to being configured as an African American expressive form. According to Rivera, "rhyming and DJing were from the beginning more ethnic-racially identified with African Americans and closed to perceived outsiders by virtue of their reliance on dexterity in the English language. Thus, they were most easily traceable to the African American oral tradition and primarily employed music considered to be Afri-an American. Hip-hop's musical dimension seems to have been premised on an Afro-diasporic urbanity, where, although the participation of young people of Caribbean ancestry was pivotal, this music was often narrowly identified solely with African Americans."[4] Rivera makes the point that the linguistic and musical dimensions of hip-hop contributed to its African Americanization because of the direct link that can be made between these dimensions and African American oral traditions and practices.

Rivera asserts that notwithstanding hip-hop's incorporation of various kinds of music, funk music is considered its musical core. This is significant because funk is widely regarded as an African American musical form and hip-hop as its heir. What are considered b-boy records, for example, are funk records. As Joseph G. Schloss points out, b-boys were getting down to funk records (and continue to do so) even before hip-hop's emergence, though he is quick to mention the presence of Latin elements in the music. This genre of music was very much an integral part of the repertoire of records b-boys danced to, further cementing the link between hip-hop and blackness.[5]

The explicit voicing of black concerns by popular MCs, coupled with the prominence of African American Vernacular English (AAVE) in rap also contributed to the racialization of hip-hop as black. Popular MCs tended to be African Americans who, in turn, articulated African American perspectives and concerns. The so-called Golden Era of hip-hop would prove to be pivotal, particularly with the popularity of Afro-centric rap in the late 1980s and early 1990s in which African American MCs led the way. It was an era marked by the popularity of so-called conscious rap or political rap that was informed by black nationalist ideology. Though the movement was short-lived, Rivera makes the point that the ascendancy of Afro-centric hip-hop would set the bounds of rap's musical contours for years to come.[6]

At the same time, AAVE remains the lingua franca of hip-hop, serving as a source of status and prestige for those who can demonstrate fluency. Hip-hop vernacular, in other words, is synonymous with African American vernacular. It is very much rooted in and an extension of African American oral traditions and practices. H. Samy Alim, for example, makes the point that hip-hop vernacular or what he describes as Hip-hop Nation Language (HHNL) "both reflects and expands the African American oral tradition."[7]

The African Americanization of hip-hop would have profound implications for the involvement of nonblack youth, compelling them to get involved in those elements of hip-hop—DJing, writing, and b-boying—that are not narrowly or more identified with blacks, as in the case of MCing. In other words, the racialization of MCing as black has left little room for nonblacks to claim a space of their own in this element of hip-hop. In the case of Puerto Rican youth, for example, Flores and Rivera suggest that the narrow identification of hip-hop with African Americans has compromised Puerto Ricans' perceived entitlement to hip-hop and obscured the pivotal role that Puerto Rican youth played in the development of hip-hop. Instead, the Puerto Rican presence in hip-hop has been commonly seen either as an intrusion into a black realm (at least until recently) or a betrayal of Puerto Ricanness, as if Puerto Ricanness and blackness are mutually exclusive categories. This kind of formulation has served to perpetuate the construction of Puerto Ricanness as distinct from blackness and has elided efforts by Puerto Rican youth to forge their own distinct identity and culture in ways that cannot be accommodated by models of cultural assimilation and loss.[8]

With regards to Filipino youth, Lakandiwa M. de Leon asserts that it is much easier to carve out a niche as a DJ, writer, or b-boy precisely because these roles are not as visible or closely scrutinized as MCing. In particular, he suggests that Filipino youth gravitate toward DJing because they are more likely to be evaluated on the basis of skills and talent rather than on race. Conversely, becoming an MC opens them up to charges of inauthenticity because of their lack of racial credentials. Filipino youth also find it difficult to pursue MCing because of the lack of Filipino MCs to emulate. As Filipino MC Kiwi puts it, "When I was in high school trying to come up as an emcee, there was no acting like a Filipino if you wanted to rap." Filipino youth, therefore, find it much easier to establish themselves as DJs, writers, and b-boys.[9]

But Rivera also points to recent shifts in the prevailing discourses of hip-hop that revolve around questions of cultural entitlement and authenticity that have served to legitimize Puerto Rican participation in hip-hop. Beginning in the 1990s, there was a marked shift in the perceived ethnoracial scope of hip-hop as the Afro-centric focus in hip-hop gave way to a ghetto-centric focus that emphasized socioeconomic realities that encompass both Puerto Ricans and blacks. Given this emphasis on what Rivera calls "class-identified blackness/nigganess,"[10] Puerto Ricans have come to be seen as core participants rather than encroachers trying to "be black."[11]

Even within the realm of MCing, we have seen a shift in the contours of authenticity and its link to blackness, encompassing what Rivera describes as the ghetto experience and, in doing so, opening up a space for non–African American groups such as Latinos to claim and achieve legitimacy.[12] In case of the underground hip-hop scene, both Jason Tanz and Anthony Kwame Harrison point to a shift in the racial demographics of MCs who inhabit this scene with the emergence of a cohort of white MCs. In contrast to previous cohorts of white MCs, today white MCs no longer feel beholden to exhibit markers of blackness as the basis of their claims to cultural legitimacy, what Tanz describes as "the age of white-on-white rhyme."[13] Instead, this group has achieved authenticity on their own terms to the extent that a white rapper is no longer an anomaly, particularly in the hip-hop underground scene.[14]

Writing as a Multiracial Phenomenon

Similar to MCing and the other elements of hip-hop, writing's emergence is rooted in the historical and structural conditions of New York City. But while it is now customary to classify writing as one of the constituent elements of hip-hop, it existed as an autonomous practice years before it came to be linked to DJing, MCing, and b-boying, as it came into being in the late 1960s and early 1970s and predated the other elements of hip-hop. This would have implications in terms of how writers themselves would view writing and its perceived racial scope in relation to the other elements of hip-hop. Thus, writers are the most vociferous when it comes to questioning the proposition that hip-hop constitutes an African American expressive form or that writing is one of the primary components of hip-hop. Accordingly, writing's status as an element of hip-hop is most questionable as compared to the other elements.

A recurring theme in both early and more recent accounts on writing is the notion that writing is the most integrated of all the elements of hip-hop. In many ways, this has become a defining feature of this expressive form and works against the notion of hip-hop as an African American expressive form. This was evident in one of the first scholarly works on writing, Craig Castleman's *Getting Up: Subway Graffiti in New York*, published in 1982: "Writers came from every race, nationality, and economic group in New York City. One graffiti organization, the Nation of Graffiti Artists (NOGA), has members representing numerous ethnic groups, including Chinese-Americans, West Indians, Ukrainians, Filipinos, Dominicans, and Nigerians. In economic background members range from sons and daughters of the wealthy to kids who live in the streets."[15] A more recent account, published almost twenty years after Castleman's book, recapitulates essentially the same theme, the notion of writing as an integrated expressive form: "Writing was among the first of a cluster of new aesthetic practices now grouped together as "hip-hop" that developed within the multiracial youth cultures of Harlem, El Barrio, the South Bronx, and central Brooklyn during the late 1960s and 1970s."[16] Jeff Chang makes a similar point: "First practiced largely by inner-city youths of color, by the mid-'70s the second generation of writers was more integrated than the army. Upper East Side whites apprenticed themselves to Bronx-based blacks. Brooklyn Ricans learned from white working class graf kings from Queens."[17] Finally, Gregory J. Snyder foregrounds how the diversity of those who have come together to make this expressive form extends beyond race: "It is important to note, however, that this cultural diversity is not a question of racial demarcation. Graffiti has always been and continues to be a racially, ethnically, and economically diverse culture. Writing is a meritocracy; it's about skills."[18] Unlike MCing, then, writing is generally configured as a multiracial expressive form rather than as an African American one. It is generally perceived as an expressive form that cuts across ethnic and racial as well as national and class lines.

As the conventional narrative of writing goes, youths of color may have dominated writing in its formative moments, but it quickly became a multiracial (and multiclassed) youth form with the involvement of youth from various ethnic, racial, and class backgrounds. The varied demographic makeup of writing culture, for instance, is foregrounded in the classic documentary

Style Wars. A white writer interviewed in the film makes the point that notwithstanding the widespread perception of writing as a black or Puerto Rican thing, it encompasses writers from a broad spectrum of ethnic, racial, and class backgrounds, and yet it is youths of color who are criminalized as thieves and vandals.[19]

It is not simply the involvement of Latino and African American youth that figures in the construction of writing as a multiracial expressive form. There is also the acknowledged role of white youth not only as practitioners but as innovators. Most celebrated is the Greek writer TAKI 183, who is credited with sparking the modern writing movement in the early 1970s. According to the conventional narrative of writing, a February 1971 *New York Times* profile not only marked the first time a writer received notoriety from the press but also inspired countless numbers of youth to pursue writing. There is also TRACY 168, less known but the founder of the seminal writing group Wanted, which became one of the largest writing groups in the mid-1970s.[20]

Cultural critics like Synder make the point that what distinguishes graffiti from the other constituent elements of hip-hop is the way it is not deeply embedded in African American cultural practices and traditions: "Unlike most indigenous forms of American music, graffiti is not specifically steeped in African-American cultural traditions, and white kids, black kids, brown kids, rich kids, and poor kids have all participated in the creation and perpetuation of graffiti culture from the beginning. Graffiti is rich in the cultural traditions of New York City urban youth, with kids from many backgrounds playing starring and supporting roles."[21] For Synder, then, such a trajectory distinguishes writing from the other constituent elements of hip-hop but also unhinges the relationship between hip-hop and blackness.

A related theme is the notion of writing as a unifying force, emerging at a time when New York was wracked by gang activity and the city was segregated along ethnic, racial, and class lines. In this kind of environment, writing served as a catalyst for unity because of the way it created camaraderie among writers. This would pave the way for the formation of writing groups or writing crews that allowed writers to transcend the kinds of divisions that marked New York in the post–World War II period.[22] According to COCO 144, "the movement broke barriers. We were at a point where after the '50s and '60s there were the gangs, and you couldn't go into a neighborhood. Neighborhoods were put into pockets like Black Harlem, Spanish Harlem, and the Upper West Bronx. This movement is something that broke negative barriers and created unity. It was a call for unity—even amongst people who weren't writers."[23] LEE expresses similar sentiments:

A lot of people don't realize the impact the writing movement had in neighborhoods, because the gangs were still around. The gangs kept neighborhoods part, the city was a jigsaw puzzle of gangs keeping turf and territorial rights. So this movement brought people together: blacks, Puerto Ricans, whites, Orientals, Polish, from the richest to the poorest, we were equals. We took the same energy that was there to stand by your block with bats or guns and flying colors all night long and used it to go painting, to create.[24]

In an era characterized by the proliferation of gangs, writing provided an alternative social formation and outlet. At the same time, it counteracted the spatialized geography of a New York defined by segregation.

Another theme in the literature contributing to the construction of writing as a multiracial expressive form is the ethos that supposedly marks the culture. According to writing-culture scholar Joe Austin, "writing culture seems to have been relatively immune to the racial polarization that marked most of the rest of the urban population. Race and class harmony was facilitated by the writers' ethical codes. In many ways, the writers who have organized a post-industrial artisanal meritocracy based on the collective evaluation of skill and effort."[25] Austin makes the point that a significant aspect of writing culture is the development of an apprenticeship system and criteria for evaluating writers' works in which the focal point is on style innovation rather than physical appearance. In those instances when racial conflicts and tensions do arise, they are regarded as an exception to a space otherwise characterized by what Austin describes above as "race and class harmony." What matters is writers paying their dues in the form of putting in long hours to hone and cultivate their writing skills. Snyder echoes Austin's contention about the meritocratic nature of writing that supersedes other considerations: "The task of writing is to saturate the city with your name and any writer who does this will get fame and respect, regardless of style, race, gender, class, age, nationality or sexuality. In its purest form, graffiti is a democratic art form that revels in the American Dream. With desire, dedication, humility, courage, toughness, and most of all hard work, anyone can potentially become a successful graffiti writers, and maybe even make a living as a result."[26] While Snyder acknowledges the continued relevance of race, he does so in very circumscribed ways.

Given the foregoing, it is not surprising that the notion of writing as an African American expressive form has proven to be a point of contention among writers. Several of the writers interviewed in *Aerosol Kingdom: Subway Painters of New York City*, for example, take issue with the conception of writing in racial and ethnic terms and especially the emphasis placed on its purported African American and Caribbean roots. These writers insist that although many of the original writers were African American and Latino, writing is better understood as a multiracial, urban phenomenon. BLADE accentuates the diversity that marked the culture in the 1970s: "The early painters were from all nationalities, and there was great camaraderie, up until maybe 1978, 1979. My original painting crew were members of the Crazy 5, which was VAMM, CRACHEE, DEATH, TULL 13 (for the Jethro Tull band), and myself, and then COMET, AJAX, people that came along with us. VAMM was Italian, CRACHEE was Jewish, TULL 13 is Yugoslavian, I am black, COMET is Italian, AJAX was Portuguese. Everybody got along, and that's what made the whole difference."[27] LADY PINK makes a similar point about writing culture: "Writers came from all ethnic backgrounds, all classes, and the police knew to look out for a group of kids who were racially diverse— those were the writers. If a group of kids was all black or white the police wouldn't bother them. Race wasn't an obstacle for a writer to join a crew, gender wasn't either."[28] The foregoing is a recurring theme, though there are also writers who subscribe to the view that writing is an African American phenomenon. One of the writers interviewed in *Aerosol Kingdom* makes the following point: "I think writing is originally a black art form. Why? Because it has soul."[29]

The proposition that writing is a constituent element of hip-hop has also not fared well, at least among some writers. Notwithstanding media representations of writing as a vital component of hip-hop, a number of writers have themselves raised the question of whether writing should even be considered part of the form. These writers do not necessarily see any connections between writing and other elements of hip-hop. In VULCAN's view:

> This culture stood alone before hip-hop was established. Writing had its own life, its own hierarchy, and its own stars. The relationship started with writers doing flyers for DJ and MC parties in the Bronx in the 1970s. But, I feel that when hip-hop came to be downtown, commercial world, when they started doing rap shows at the Roxy and Danceteria, and art shows in galleries like the Fun Gallery, writing became linked to hip-hop music as a backdrop. . . . Since then, people think of writing as ambiance to the music, and that bothers me, because writing is a self-contained, complete form that needs no accompaniment. Writing may be an element of hip-hop, but hip-hop is not necessarily an element of writing.[30]

For LADY PINK, the purported link between writing and DJing, MCing, and breaking was more a media fabrication than an organic phenomenon that arose from a "natural" affinity between writing and other elements of hip-hop: "Wild Style [1982] was the first film that linked rap music, break-dance, and graffiti, which basically have nothing to do with each other, except that some rappers and break-dancers did graffiti on the side. But if they were also involved in rapping or break-dancing, they were not full-time, or blood writers. So the movie linked it together, now basically everybody in the world believes that most writers are either from the inner city, from the ghetto, black and Puerto Rican, but white is never really discussed."[31] Many of the writers who subscribe to this point of view point to the media as playing a key role in the perpetuation of the notion of hip-hop as an integrated set of practices. In other words, it was through films like *Wild Style* that writing became known as the visual element of hip-hop. These films naturalized and rendered organic the links among the various elements of hip-hop.

Breaking as a "Ghetto" and Puerto Rican Thing

In both popular and academic accounts, breaking is widely considered the physical manifestation of hip-hop culture. It tends to be represented more as a "street"- or "ghetto"- based expressive form rather than exclusively an African American one and is more specifically an expressive form associated with Puerto Rican youth. A recurring theme is that African American youth may very well have been its earliest practitioners, and a number of the moves may very well share "families of resemblance" with a number of African American dances (e.g., the Lindy hop, the Charleston, and the cakewalk) but it was Puerto Rican youth who immersed themselves in the art form and took it seriously at a time when their African American counterparts looked at it more as a fad: "After developing the dance for over five years, many blacks grew tired of breaking and had stopped by 1978. Some got into the Hustle or the Freak. Others did the Electric Boogie, a robotic mimelike dance popular in California and down South. However, the Puerto Ricans were just getting into breaking and had no intention of giving it up."[32] In Chang's *Can't Stop, Won't Stop*, we see a similar account: "See, the jams back then were still close to 90 percent African-American, as were most of the earliest b-boys, but they took breaking more like a phase, a fad. I say this because I had to see the reactions on their faces when we started doing it. They were like, 'Yo, breaking is played out' whenever the Hispanics would do it."[33] Beginning in the 1970s, it was Puerto Rican youth who gravitated toward breaking in significant numbers, and shortly after, they came to dominate the art form. Accordingly, the more prominent b-boy crews such as the Dynamic Rockers, the New York City Breakers, and the Rock Steady Crew came to comprise mostly Puerto Rican youth.

It was not just the significant presence of Puerto Rican youth, however, that worked against the notion of breaking as an exclusively African American space. There was also the question of breaking's perceived genealogy that exceeded the bounds of African American culture. According to Rivera, breaking "was visibly nourished by Caribbean Latino dance forms such as rumba, mambo, the Latin hustle, and rocking. Furthermore, Puerto Ricans had been and were still key in the development of the b-boy/b-girl dance style; most of the better-known breaking crews (Rock Steady Crew, the Furious Rockers, Dynamic Rockers, New York City Breakers) were primarily Puerto Rican. All of these factors made it less tenable for Boricuas to be left out of the equation in breaking."[34] As a consequence, the question of cultural legitimacy and entitlement did not become an issue the way it did within the realm of DJing and MCing. In other words, it became much more difficult to see b-boying strictly in terms of African Americanness. Accordingly, Puerto Ricans did not feel compelled to justify their presence in a purportedly African American expressive form or to compromise their Puerto Ricanness in any way.[35]

Schloss makes a similar argument, asserting that the development of this expressive form took place among small groups of working-class black and Latino youth. More broadly, he makes the claim that "even the music that gave birth to the dance is notable for its fusion of cultural elements drawn from both African American and Latino musical traditions, including Latin percussions and song structure, African American melodic and vocal techniques, and an overall aesthetic that speaks to the struggles and aspirations of urban youth of the early 1970s."[36] In his view, b-boying is very much a function of what he describes as "the clear fusion of African American and Latino cultural outlooks."[37] What this suggests for Schloss is the need to take a broader, more Afro-diasporic approach to dance given its complex genealogy and varied influences.

Additionally, Rivera speculates that breaking's short-lived commercial rise and dramatic fall in the mid-1980s may have also worked against its African Americanization. Like rap (and other elements of hip-hop), breaking generated a good deal of media exposure in the early 1980s, with b-boys appearing in a number of commercials, television shows, and films and performing in such global spectacles as the 1984 Olympics in Los Angeles.[38] Just as quickly as breaking became both a national and international dance sensation, public and commercial interest in the art form sharply declined, fulfilling media pronouncements that breaking was simply a fad (the media made similar kinds of pronouncement in relation to rap) and leaving a number of b-boys feeling exploited and disillusioned. Frosty Freeze reflected: "We were just kids, all caught up in that fame and fortune. . . . We didn't know much about the business."[39] Ken Swift echoes Frosty Freeze's sentiments: "When you're young, you're not thinking like a historian, that this could be damaging to your culture. It flew over our heads."[40] Vince "Mr. Animation" Foster even envisioned striking it rich: "When I was in *Breakin'* I thought I was a big star, making $100 a day."[41] Had breaking enjoyed the same sustained commercial viability and appeal as MCing, Rivera speculates that it too could have been racialized as an African American form because of the perceived profitability of blackness.[42]

DJ Culture, Race, and Filipino DJs

DJing would enjoy popular and commercial attention about a decade after breaking and writing peaked in its popularity. Like breaking and writing, it would be racialized as a multiracial expressive form.

And like these other expressive forms, DJing has come to be configured as being informed by an ethos of collegiality and collaboration that serves as a unifying force on a global scale.[43] Notwithstanding these parallels, however, DJ culture's racialization history and trajectory would prove to be distinctive in many ways, particularly in terms of the place considered to be the mecca of DJ innovation and the identity of its acknowledged innovators.

The peak of DJing's popularity in the late 1980s and early 1990s paved the way for the publication of a spate of books on DJ culture, focusing not just on hip-hop but DJ culture as a whole, encompassing multiple genres of music. These publications include Bill Brewster and Frank Broughton's *Last Night a DJ Saved My Life: The History of the Disc Jockey*, Kurt B. Reighley's *Looking for the Perfect Beat: The Art and Culture of the DJ*, Ulf Poshardt's *DJ Culture*, and Luke Crisell, Phil White, and Rob Principe's *On the Record: The Scratch DJ Academy Guide*. For the most part, these accounts tend to provide the same kind of narrative that takes a celebratory tone toward DJs and traces their fall and return to prominence. In these accounts, the underlying assumption is that DJing constitutes an African American or Afro-diasporic expressive form that has now evolved into an inclusive one. A substantive consideration of race, however, is largely lacking. Instead, a point of emphasis is on the broadening racial scope of DJ culture and how it constitutes a racially integrated expressive form. Ultimately, these accounts provide deracialized accounts of DJ culture even as a number of them trace the origins and influences of DJing within the context of African American culture.[44]

Similar to writing, DJing is configured as a unifying force on a global scale that mitigates against a reading of DJing in race-specific terms. As the authors of *On the Record* put it, "DJing is a uniting force that brings together people from all backgrounds in a celebration of music."[45] A focal point is on the spirit of collegiality and collaboration that suffuses the culture and informs relations among DJs. It is a fairly common practice among DJs, for example, to collaborate or to contribute to one another's work.

With the rise of a handful of DJs to superstar status, accounts of DJ culture aim to demystify the aura that has come to surround DJs. In a number of these accounts, then, a focal point is an ethos of populism that supposedly permeates the culture: "But the idea that DJing is only for a select and privileged few is just a myth. The truth is everyone is a DJ."[46] The construction of DJing in populist terms is typically pitted against the purported elitism that has come to permeate MCing and typify MCs, who are perceived as being totally out of touch with consumers and fans of hip-hop.

In these accounts, DJs are represented as embodying the very essence of hip-hop, particularly at a time when the culture was stagnant and MCs have seemingly lost their way: "The turntablists shunned the mainstream hip-hop scene that had left DJs out in the cold in the late '80s and early '90s, preferring to focus on technical innovation and a spirit of community that stayed true to the founding principles of the genre."[47] The foregoing references a movement within DJing that came about in part as a response to the marginalization of DJs.

A recurrent theme is the significance of the Bay Area in the evolution of DJ culture and in particular its pivotal role in the emergence of turntablism. Kurt B. Reighley reports: "In the early '90s, the Bay Area of California began to emerge as a hotbed for innovative DJs and the notion of turntablism coalesced more clearly. Distanced from the mainstream hip-hop communities of Los Angeles and the East Coast, and blessed with a tradition of ambitious independent music, the San Francisco region hosted a wealth of mobile party DJs during the mid-80s, and local battle culture was fertile with talent."[48] Honing their skills in relative obscurity and in an environment that Reighley describes as outside the "mainstream hip-hop" world, Bay Area DJs would create a movement that fundamentally transformed DJ culture and turned the Bay Area into a DJ mecca.

The widely acknowledged role of the Bay Area in the evolution of DJing would prove to be consequential in the construction of DJing as a racially transcendent space given the region's reputation for cultivating a thriving independent hip-hop scene that may not get a lot of commercial airplay but nonetheless boasts a global fan base. A common refrain you hear from Bay Area artists is the freedom and control that comes with independence from major labels. According to Bay Area DJ Peanut Butter Wolf, "one of the Bay Area's distinctive features is how it's all done independently. It's more work but you can control your art."[49] Domino, Hiero producer and manager, agrees: "It gives you a lot of freedom. For example you can go in and record a song today and release it next week not like a major."[50] For many Bay Area artists, the absence of major label affiliation has become a source of pride, an asset rather than liability that serves to open up creative possibilities.

A hallmark of the Bay Area hip-hop scene is the unity among Bay Area artists fostered by their commitment to originality, creativity, and self-reliance. It is a scene in which local artists often work with one another and with like-minded artists outside the area, or appear on one another's albums, or appear together to do shows. Another hallmark of the Bay Area hip-hop scene is the diversity of sounds that has redefined and expanded the bounds of West Coast hip-hop beyond the gangsta rap of the 1980s. To illustrate, independent labels such as ABB Records and Stones Throw boast rosters of artists that cannot be reduced to a particular sound or style.[51]

But it's not just the diversity of sound and style that has come to mark the Bay Area hip-hop scene. This scene has also come to be known for its racial diversity, giving rise to what Anthony Kwame Harrison describes as a particular kind of ideal: "Within the world of Bay Area underground hip-hop, a professed colorblind mantra is celebrated. This ideal is upheld even in the face of frequent race-based assessments of hip-hop legitimacy."[52] Harrison goes on to assert that "within such a racially diverse metropolitan setting, where subcultural affiliations are at times more strongly felt than race, one result is an inclusive ideology of hip-hop (racial) participation that counters commercial rap music's near complete reliance on black performers."[53] Within this scene, then, hip-hop legitimacy is not predicated on exhibiting markers of blackness. Rather, a premium is placed on what Harrison describes as a "discourse of racial democracy and egalitarianism."[54] The implication here is that the hip-hop scene in the Bay Area is not as susceptible to being influenced by the imperatives of commodity culture and its valorization of blackness because of the ethos of independence that permeates it. In effect, the Bay Area hip-hop scene provides a counterpoint to the perceived and purported blackness of hip-hop.

The role of non–African American DJs in the evolution of DJ culture would also prove to be consequential in the configuration of DJing in race-neutral terms. In the case of Filipino DJs, they usually enter the picture in the late 1980s and early 1990s, coinciding with the resurgence of DJing and specifically the emergence of turntablism, though their involvement in DJing predates

this period. They may not have been the first DJs to realize the musical potential and possibilities of turntables, but nonetheless, it is generally acknowledged that Filipino DJs were at the forefront of the turntablist movement,
leading the way in pushing the sonic boundaries of DJing and advancing the
notion of turntables as musical instruments.

Accordingly, primarily Filipino American groups like ISP have come to be
valorized for purportedly embodying the "true" essence of hip-hop. As Neva
Chonin puts it: "They're the heroes in a way. After a decade of gangsta rap,
which celebrated cash and violence, they've brought back the original tenets
of hip-hop: community, creativity, and above all fun."[55] In keeping with deracialized accounts of DJ culture, however, Filipinoness is configured as a difference that does not make a difference, a dynamic recapitulated in the film
Scratch (dir. Doug Pray, 2001), a documentary on DJ culture.

Scratch, DJ Culture, and Difference

Originally released in 2001, *Scratch* explores the culture and art of DJing and
touches on many of the same themes articulated in popular accounts of DJ
culture. Interweaving performance footage with interviews with prominent
and influential hip-hop DJs, including a number of prominent Filipino DJs, the
film provides a primer on the history of DJing, tracing the origins of the scratch
and documenting the different aspects of DJ culture from turntablism to beat
digging. Similar to hip-hop documentaries like *Style Wars* and *Planet B-Boy*,
viewers get to hear from the practitioners themselves—in this case, what got
them into DJing, their influences, and their views on the future of DJing.

Part of the underlying narrative of the film revolves around the decline and
subsequent resurgence of DJs. DJs occupied center stage in hip-hop before MCs
supplanted them as the focal point of the culture. Instead, as a number of DJs
interviewed in the film point out, DJs were rendered expendable as MCs rose in
the early 1980s sparked by the mass commodification of rap and concurrent
developments in sound technology that made DJs less important. Afrika Bambaataa, for example, makes the following point in the film: "The DJs are the
ones that put the MCs out there, but then the MCs became the power; a lot of
MCs got away from the cultural part and got into 'all about the benjamins,'
and uh they left the DJ behind."[56] The shift of power from the DJ to the MC
coincided with the decline of hip-hop culture, and yet it was the DJ who would
revitalize the culture and hip-hop as a whole by remaining true to its founding principles, including remaining dedicated to elevating the art of DJing.

Though competition is stressed in the film as an integral aspect of DJ culture,
a spirit of collegiality and collaboration marks the atmosphere constructed

by the film, a spirit that cuts across generational lines, with each generation of DJs preserving and passing on the legacies of DJing to the next generation. Echoing the significance of crews in b-boying and writing, the film underscores the significance of DJ crews and the functions they serve, including allowing DJs to pool resources and learn from one another. The film also emphasizes an ideology of meritocracy, namely the countless hours and dedication it takes to be a good DJ that serves to demystify DJing. As Rob Swift alludes in the film, it takes months of practice and preparation for a six-minute routine at a DJ competition like the DMC.

Filipino DJs are an undeniable presence in the film, with the director, Doug Pray, highlighting the contributions and innovations of Filipino DJs like Q-Bert and Mix Master Mike, and those of predominantly Filipino DJ crews like the Beat Junkies without necessarily foregrounding their Filipinoness. Rachel Devitt makes the point, however, that notwithstanding the significant contributions of Filipinos to the evolution of DJing, "the particularly *Filipino American* history of DJ culture and the considerable contributions of Filipino artists to hip-hop as a whole" remains obscured.[57] One could argue, therefore, that the film's focus on Filipino DJs is exceptional in that it represents a rupture in conventional accounts of pop music and hip-hop that render Filipinos illegible. It provides a corrective to accounts that elides what Devitt describes as "the legacy of Filipino Americans" in hip-hop that has yet to be fully recognized and acknowledged.[58]

In the hip-hop universe constructed by *Scratch*, however, Pray subsumes "the particularly *Filipino American* history of DJ culture" under an integrationist logic that serves to render regional and racial affiliations irrelevant. In the words of the filmmaker himself, *Scratch* "is the most diverse film I've ever seen. And as the director I did nothing to make it so. That's one difference between underground hip-hop and mainstream rap. It wasn't about East Coast versus West Coast, it wasn't about black vs. white."[59] Pray thus echoes and appeals to a particular narrative that has come to be associated with the hip-hop underground scene, a narrative informed by the transcendence of race. He subscribes to a kind of integrationist logic in which DJ culture thrives precisely because of its disavowal of difference in contradistinction to "mainstream" hip-hop predicated on the valorization of blackness.

Filipino youth involvement in hip-hop has not been confined to DJing, yet it is within this element of hip-hop that they have left an indelible mark. In the next chapter, I delineate the various authenticating strategies Filipino DJs rely on in order to cave out a niche and establish cultural legitimacy within DJ culture.

Chapter 3   **"The Scratching Is What Got Me Hooked"**

Filipino American DJs in the Bay Area

FILIPINO YOUTH INVOLVEMENT WITHIN DJING only makes sense in relation to the cultural landscape of the Bay Area. It is very much a function of developments specific to the region at a particular historical juncture. In particular, the DJs I interviewed were very much influenced, one way or the other, by the burgeoning mobile DJ scene that took hold of the Bay Area in the 1980s, although my respondents did not get into DJing until well after the peak of that scene. In this chapter, I provide a profile of Filipino DJs I interviewed and shed light on the nature of their engagement with DJing.

In many ways, the DJs featured here come from families that fit the profile of recent Filipino migrants to the United States, in that, compared to earlier groups of Filipino immigrants, they are marked by greater class and gender stratification with the influx of professionals and highly skilled workers and female migrants. Filipina nurses, for example, constituted a significant percentage of contemporary Filipino migrants to the United States. As Paul Ong and Tania Azores suggest, the Philippines has been the major supplier of foreign-trained nurses working in the United States; at least twenty-five thousand Filipino nurses migrated to the United States between 1966 and 1985. Given the prominence of this group, then, it is not surprising that the mothers of three of my respondents are nurses.[1] But while a number of my respondents come from relatively privileged occupational and educational backgrounds, the class status of others is a bit more ambiguous. Class background in the Philippines, in other words, did not necessarily translate into the same class background in the United States.

My interviews with Filipino DJs were organized around a set of themes—what drew them to the culture, how they came up with their DJ names, and how DJing figured in their career plans. I asked my respondents about how their families viewed their involvement in hip-hop as a way to accentuate the gendered dimensions of DJ culture. I also queried them about how they conceived

33

of the racial scope of hip-hop—whether they considered hip-hop an African American expressive form or something else. One of the questions I asked my respondents is whether or not they considered DJing part of Filipino culture and on what basis. I was especially interested in how they conceived of the relationship between DJ culture and Filipino culture.[2]

Study Participants

Deeandroid was born in Oakland, California, in 1980. Her parents were born in the Philippines but met in Iran, where her mother worked as a nurse and her father was studying to be an aircraft mechanic. They immigrated to the United States in the late 1970s, first to Oakland and then to nearby Vallejo, where many of their relatives already lived. This speaks to the significance of transnational networks to Filipino migration and in particular, the dependence of migrants on kin already in the United States for assistance with their settlement and adaptation, including information about jobs, housing, and schooling for their children. Deeandroid's parents continue to hold the same jobs in the United States that they'd held in other countries. She has an older brother who is also a mechanic and an older sister who is attending nursing school. At the time of the interview, Deeandroid was working at a public relations company as an office administration assistant. She is also a student at San Francisco State University (SFSU), where she majors in business.[3]

In terms of class background, my respondents appear to come from relatively privileged occupational and educational backgrounds. Rygar was born in San Jose, California, in 1981. His parents were born in the Philippines; his mother in Pangasinan and his father in Ilocos. They met in the United States at the University of Washington, although Rygar is unsure of the circumstances. In California, Rygar's parents first lived in Fremont before moving to Union City, where Rygar spent his formative years. His father is a physician at Kaiser while his mother is a registered nurse who left the profession in order to take care of Rygar and his three younger sisters. He is a student at UC Berkeley where he also teaches a class on the basics of DJing.[4]

Rey-Jun was born in San Francisco, California, in 1974. His parents were born in the Philippines and immigrated to the United States in the late 1960s. They first settled in Daly City, California, before they moved to Concord in the late 1970s. Rey-Jun's father graduated from SFSU with a degree in health science and has worked at the department store Macy's for about twenty-five years as a supervisor, while his mother was a nurse in both the Philippines and the United States. His father continues to work at Macy's, whereas his mother runs four convalescent homes—one in Milpitas and three

in Concord. Rey-Jun has been attending Diablo Valley College (DVC) inter-
mittently, where he has taken administrative and business classes in preparation for taking over the family business.[5]

While it appears that a number of my respondents come from relatively
privileged occupational and educational backgrounds, the class status of some
of my respondents is a bit more difficult to peg. Statistix was born in the
Philippines and immigrated to the United States at the age of three in 1987
with his mother and older sibling. His father did not rejoin the family until
1997, ten years after the family first immigrated to the United States. Upon
arrival in California, they rented an apartment in San Francisco and eventually purchased their own home in the Portola District. His father works as a
transporter at both Stanford University and at General Hospital but also
works in maintenance at the State Building while his mother works for admis-
sions at the University of California, San Francisco (UCSF), and as a front
desk clerk at a Best Western Hotel.[6]

Celskiii was born in Chicago in 1980 but grew up in Vallejo. Her family
first immigrated to Norfolk, Virginia, from which they moved to Chicago so
that they could be close to relatives. The family eventually moved to and settled in Vallejo, where many of their relatives already lived. Celskiii self-identifies
as coming from a working-class background. Her father does food service at
a hospital, while her mother works at the post office. Celskiii has an older sister
who is in dental school in Ohio and a younger brother in Los Angeles. Currently a student at SFSU, Celskiii also tutors fifth graders and works with at-
risk students at Balboa High School in San Francisco.[7]

Tease was born in San Jose, California, in 1981. Her parents were born in
the Philippines and immigrated to the United States in the late 1970s. Tease's
mother first immigrated to the United States in 1977 and was followed by her
husband two years later, a period Tease describes as especially difficult for her
mother. Tease now lives in San Francisco in order to be closer to SFSU, where
she is majoring in marketing. She has a younger brother who also attends
SFSU and lives with her.[8]

In Tease's case, a fortuitous set of events enabled her family to achieve
upward social mobility at a time when the family was barely eking out a living. Tease's father was a bank teller in the Philippines, a job he also held when
he first arrived in the United States, while her mother was a chemistry teacher
in the Philippines and worked graveyard shifts at a chemistry lab in the United
States. Tease readily admits that the family's first few years in the United States
were a struggle:

INTERVIEWER: Owning and managing a store, is that something your parents always wanted to do?

TEASE: We were struggling financially. I remember that. We were eating, like, corned beef everyday and I was just like "What is this?" . . . They were financially struggling and the [Filipino grocery] store has been in our family since 1981, and actually even prior to that. My uncle, who came here first, he came here first and then he passed it down to his younger brother who passed it down to us. . . . I mean he loved the store—don't get me wrong—but he fell in love with this great aunt of mine, and it's like "Oh, screw that. I want a family. Here you go. You can have the store." It was really big for my parents then.[9]

According to Tease, her parents no longer have to worry about money after taking over the store. They now have the means to live comfortably and do whatever it is they want, like investing in property and traveling all around the globe.

One Tyme was born in San Francisco, California, in 1982. Her parents were born in the Philippines and immigrated to the United States in their teens. They first settled in San Francisco and have been there since the late 1970s. Her father is a bellboy at a Holiday Inn while her mother is an accountant. The only child in the family, One Tyme is a student at UC Berkeley, where she majors in ethnic studies and teaches a class on the basics of DJing.[10]

Soup-a-Crunk was born in San Francisco, California, in 1979. Like my other respondents, his parents were born in the Philippines. The family immigrated to the United States in 1978 and initially settled in San Francisco in order to be close to relatives—an uncle and grandparents—before they moved to Oakland, a recurrent pattern among my respondents. Soup-a-Crunk's father is a tailor while his mother works for the air quality management district. Soup-a-Crunk is the youngest of six children and is the only one of them born in the United States. One sister works at a law firm and another works with his mother in air quality management. Soup-a-Crunk also has three older brothers—one is a mechanic and machinist, another is a security guard, and the third works at Home Depot. He graduated from UC Berkeley and plans to pursue a career in film.[11]

Entry into DJ Culture

For my respondents, growing up in a DJ mecca like the Bay Area meant spending their formative years around DJs who introduced them to DJing at an early age and encouraged them to become DJs themselves. Cousins, friends, and neighbors already into DJing proved to have had a profound influence on their decision to become DJs.

STATISTIX: I was about fourteen years old. It was that summer, a whole bunch of parties was going on. But then I was kind of young so I wasn't into clubs yet. What happened was that I started meeting some other people, people older than me that had interest in DJing. There was one friend that stands out in high school. He asked me if I was a DJ; I just told him I was interested in music and I was thinking about DJing as a hobby. That's when he took me to his house and that's where we started. And I saw his turntables and I had no idea what the best turntables look like. All I know was what a turntable looks like, so that when I got to his house he told me to go ahead and mess with them. But I had no idea. I didn't even know how to turn it on. It's not just a light switch that you turn on. It's like a whole bunch of these other gadgets you gotta know how to operate.[12]

One Tyme and Celskiii recount similar experiences of following the lead of their relatives already into DJing.

ONE TYME: It was like in the eighth grade when I first got my first set. I was still really young, like around ten, and my cousins used to do it in my garage, you know, house DJs. They've like the lights and all that flashing, and put up the sound system and I'll just be there. I finally asked my parents for some turntables.[13]

CELSKIII: The sound, the music. Just like when I was little and I used to see cousins mix and stuff, I mean the fact that they could get everyone dancing with the music. I couldn't articulate that but I knew that there was something cool about that when I was little. And also, when we go to garage parties, there would be b-boy battles, DJs were the people I watched. I don't know. It's just like music. I guess it was something I felt. And the scratching, the scratching especially is what really got me hooked.[14]

Even before they had a full grasp of what it takes and what it means to be a DJ, my respondents got a taste of the power and influence of DJs in terms of controlling and taking command of the crowd and the potential of DJing in terms of creating new music. These experiences, in turn, became the basis for their involvement in DJ culture.

DJing is a craft, and like any other craft, it comes with its own set of techniques, skills, and procedures. Aspiring DJs, therefore, need to familiarize themselves with the tools of the trade—what turntables to use, which ones are more suited to mixing as opposed to battling, which are the best mixers, what are the most durable needles, and so forth. Acquiring this knowledge usually involves having to go through some sort of apprenticeship with more established and more experienced DJs—typically older peers and relatives—who serve as mentors and teach these respondents not only the basics of DJing but also "tricks" or "secrets" of the trade. Statistix recalls some information he learned from an older DJ: "He was just telling me that every time you have a gig, bring two girls. I said, 'Why is that?' Because when you first play your song and it's a good song, don't waste it. Have those two dance to open up the dance floor. I was like, 'Oh, okay. Always bring two girls.' So he started sharing his secrets with me. I had nothing to share with him because I did not really have that much experience."[15] The other DJs I interviewed recounted similar stories of more-experienced individuals teaching them the nuances of DJing and what it takes to become a good DJ even before they got hold of their own equipment. The kind of apprenticeship experienced by my respondents echoes a similar kind of arrangement in other elements of hip-hop, such as writing.[16] Additionally, these experiences foreground the importance of social networks as a way for experienced DJs to pass on musical knowledge and expertise, and for novice DJs to initially make their mark.

Although my respondents got into DJing at a time when the mobile DJ scene was in decline, they point to it as an important influence in their decision to pursue DJing. This is not a surprise given that many of their older peers and relatives were part of the mobile DJ scene. Statistix, for example, considers the well-known mobile DJ crew Style Beyond Compare (SBC) a big influence in his development as a DJ:

> STATISTIX: SBC is like my idol, man. Those guys are too good. I remember when I first heard their cd, it's like, "Damn, I wish I could do that. I wish I could be like them," 'cause I already got past saying to myself, "Oh, I wish I could be a DJ like them." But it's now, "I wish I can do the things that they can do." I mean, they're known. They are like known for the way they mix. And then they're doing gigs that's like two thousand dollars in one night. It just blows me away that they could make a CD like that. It sounds like they're on twenty turntables at the same time and I just wish I could do that too.[17]

Likewise, Celskiii recounts the influence of the mobile DJ scene on her development as a DJ:

> INTERVIEWER: Were you influenced by the DJ mobile scene as well?
> CELSKIII: Oh yeah. When I was little, seeing them, my cousins who were in some of the crews, seeing it, that's when I realized DJs have power 'cause they're controlling the party. It influenced me in the sense that I saw that.[18]

The mobile DJ scene not only gave my respondents a sense of the power and possibilities of DJing but also a group of DJs to emulate in terms of their status, prestige, and skills. More broadly, the influence of a mobile DJ crew like SBC speaks to how the DJs I interviewed were part of a tradition that was already well established by the time they got into DJing.

In Rey-Jun's case, the influence of the DJ mobile scene was more direct. He was a member of a DJ crew called Sounds Mystically Divine, a mobile DJ group that generally performed gigs at high school and house parties playing mostly hi-NRG music and hip-hop. According to Rey-Jun, the aim of the crew was not necessarily to make money but to get their name out and earn some recognition among peers:

INTERVIEWER: So at seventh grade you were already part of a DJ crew?
REY-JUN: Yeah.
INTERVIEWER: What did you guys do?
REY-JUN: We just did parties.
INTERVIEWER: What was your crew name?
REY-JUN: Sounds Mystically Divine.
INTERVIEWER: Did you guys get to do high school parties as well?
REY-JUN: Basically junior high, some house parties and stuff like that. We go to a lot of house parties. We did a couple of school dances for junior high.
INTERVIEWER: What kind of music did you guys play?
REY-JUN: A lot of high energy, Miami bass and hip-hop.
INTERVIEWER: So at the time it was all about mobile DJs.
REY-JUN: Yeah, like Imagine and all that. It was kind of cool because back then you were so young and you go to watch all those crews battle. It was something to look at. Those battles were mostly like quick mix battles.
INTERVIEWER: Did you guys participate in the battles?
REY-JUN: No, we didn't participate.
INTERVIEWER: Why not? Were you guys intimidated?
REY-JUN: No. I guess you can say the goal of the crew was to get to know people, to get your name on that flyer, to get some kind of name recognition for your crew.[19]

Rey-Jun not only started out as a mobile DJ in the late 1980s, but he also attended Imagine-sponsored events that exposed him to the competitive aspect of DJing as well as what it took for a crew to make a name for itself.[20]

Invariably, my respondents all point to Q-Bert, a renowned and influential Pinoy DJ who grew up in the Bay Area, as a galvanizing figure who transformed the way they look at DJing and foregrounded its creative possibilities. After watching and hearing Q-Bert perform, for example, Deeandroid and Celskiii no longer viewed DJing in quite the same way:

DEEANDROID: Like, really really attracted me? It's that show in '97, *Planet Rock* with Shortkut, Q, and Mike. You know, I was always exposed to hip-hop because my older brother and sister were into it and we had our own dance group before. But I never really looked at DJing the way I did when I saw them that night. Like, seeing them that night, seeing them perform, as a group, their energy, that was like, like it really spoke to me but you know I did not really know it then. I was just so amazed by it. But after that, you know, that was the beginning of being addicted to it almost.[21]

CELSKIII: I got my turntables at first to mix. But then I realized or thought it was boring. And then when you saw Q-Bert and them perform, I was like, "Oh." From that moment on, that's when everything changed. I don't know, something about playing it. It feels good when you can scratch and stuff. I don't know. I understood it even though I did not really understand what scratches they were doing. And the patterns, I heard the patterns. I heard the rhythm and the rhythm is, I guess, what caught me. I just wanted to be able to play rhythms.[22]

That Q-Bert was Filipino also made a difference and helped to further enhance his appeal among my respondents. In the following, One Tyme references a line uttered by Babu in the documentary *Scratch*, a line that resonates with a number of my respondents, while Celskiii alludes to the undeniable presence of Filipino DJs as making a huge difference in her decision to pursue DJing:

ONE TYME: Yeah, that's all I knew was Q-Bert. I just seen the movie *Scratch* and Babu said, he was like, Filipinos don't have many role models—it's your parents and Q-Bert. And I was like yeah, that is basically true, because there aren't many in the media, Filipino role models. . . . Like, I always watch his videos, the DMC Finals, and all that.[23]

INTERVIEWER: Did it make a difference that many of these DJs you're talking about are Filipinos in terms of your involvement?

CELSKIII: Yeah, like later, when I first learned about Q-Bert and them, I was just like, "Wow, they're Filipino." Of course, that made me feel like, "Oh, this is something I could do too." And plus growing up, there's a bunch of Filipino DJs. It's like something that was already practiced within the Filipino community.[24]

Given the persistent absence of Filipino role models, Q-Bert serves as a source of inspiration among the DJs I interviewed not only because of the way he pushed the boundaries of DJing but also because of the visibility he brought to Filipino youth.

For as long as my respondents could remember, hip-hop has been a big part of their lives, an expressive form they can get into at an early age. In many instances, my respondents' involvement in DJing was preceded by their involvement in other elements of hip-hop:

INTERVIEWER: Let's talk about hip-hop in general. What attracted you to hip-hop? What is it about hip-hop that you find so appealing?

REY-JUN: I think it's the whole culture, the whole aspect of it is basically what attracted me to hip-hop, 'cause when I was young I tried to break and stuff, and that did not work. I don't know. I was amazed by all the graffiti and just the music behind it. Yeah, I guess it's basically the whole culture of the whole thing—hanging out with your friends, trying to decipher songs, lyrics.[25]

For Rey-Jun, it was not specifically DJing that attracted him to hip-hop but the whole culture itself. He looks to hip-hop as an integrated set of activities that are not simply interchangeable with rapping.

In Deeandroid's case, she started out as a b-girl in a dance crew, thanks in large part to her siblings, who exposed her to hip-hop at an early age. She mentioned that at the time, there were a lot of b-boy crews and nothing else to do in Vallejo. Dancing appealed to her not only because it was something many of her peers were into but also because it was an accessible cultural practice.[26] Likewise, Soup-a-Crunk started out as an MC and as a b-boy before he got into DJing. In high school, he used to write rhymes and perform for different high schools as well as break under the name "G-Force." For Soup-a-Crunk, hip-hop was not something he consciously set out to participate in but just something he did with many of his peers.[27]

In some cases, my respondents gravitated toward DJing in part because they were not very good at the other elements of hip-hop:

INTERVIEWER: Could you talk about your involvement in DJing?
REY-JUN: I was always into music even when I was young. I got into DJing probably when I was, like, in seventh grade. I was part of a DJ crew. . . . I always loved music and I could not break. I tried breaking but I could not break for shit. So yeah, my friends decided they wanted to start up a DJ crew, and that show I got into it.[28]

In Statistix's case, he was involved in both b-boying and writing before he became a DJ. He tried breaking but quickly realized that he was not very good at it:

STATISTIX: Well everything that you just mentioned right now, the only thing I did not do was rapping. Breakdancing, I've to give props to one of my other friends, BJ. He was from Mission High. This dude, he'll come to my house weekends and teach me how to break. We'll make videos and stuff. He would come to my house weekends and we'll just start breakdancing and put a video camera on, put a strobe light on. But it was not the thing for me because I started doing those "crabs" and those "head spins" and I was not good at all. After a while, trying so much, my wrists started hurting, I knew it wasn't for me.[29]

And although Statistix does not consider himself a graffiti artist, he knows how to do pieces.[30] It is something he has done and continues to do ever since elementary school mainly on regular white paper.

Ultimately, however, my respondents were drawn to DJing by the music, power, and energy of DJ culture as well as the creative possibilities it affords. A number of them point to a "feeling," "vibe," or "rush" unique to DJ culture that comes from eliciting a strong, positive response from the crowd. This involves the build-up and subsequent release of tension through the careful selection of records, what one author has described as "peaks" within the context of underground dance music.[31]

> ONE TYME: It's like, I got a gig, I'm rocking the party, and it's like the crowd is just feeling your vibe and they're singing every lyric to the song you're playing. And they're like responding to you, not even having an MC. They're screaming when the first break comes on and they're like "Yeah." It's like that feeling is the best feeling in the world. I could never get it anywhere else.[32]
>
> TEASE: The biggest rush that you could get as a DJ, or the biggest satisfaction is, like, looking at the crowd having fun, me spinning at a club, when you get a crowd response from a record, it's like the best thing. It's like, "Wow, I'm making these people happy. Who am I? I'm just a little nobody." But honestly, in reality, you being a DJ, regardless of male or female, it's your job to make them happy. You don't play what you want to hear. I mean it's cool and it's your own taste in fashion, but being a DJ, your job is to play what they want to hear.[33]

But being a good DJ is not just about playing what the crowd wants but also knowing what to play at just the right moment. Rygar explains:

> RYGAR: The crowd, what they know is the transitions that a DJ makes. Like, if they're clean, like you basically want to make the transition smooth so that the crowd won't be like, "Oh, what just happened," you know. So that and playing what the crowd wants, playing the song after another, you know, not playing all hype songs at the same time but keeping a good balance so you could eventually peak at the end of the party it will be so high that it will end and [the crowd] be like, "Damn, that was fun," you know.[34]

For my respondents, then, much of the appeal of DJing stems from being in a position to move the crowd and generate a feeling or vibe they do not get elsewhere. It enables them to exercise agency and control in a way that is foreclosed in other spheres of their lives.

In Rey-Jun's case, he got into DJing in the late 1980s, a time when the mobile DJ scene was in decline, but also when turntablism was just beginning to emerge. This transition is significant because it changed Rey-Jun's perception of what it means to be a DJ:

> INTERVIEWER: You mentioned how an emphasis on the skills got you into DJing even more. Can you talk more about that?

REY-JUN: Because it's a new concept. It wasn't just mixing records anymore. You were actually trying to make sounds, you know, playing with records. It was like playing an instrument, you can say.

INTERVIEWER: How did that change your perception of yourself as a DJ?

REY-JUN: 'Cause it wasn't about the girls or any of that shit, you know what I mean? It wasn't about that. It was about being creative and being original and trying to figure out what you can do on your own. It's like trying to be innovative.[35]

For Rey-Jun, DJing was no longer simply a matter of mixing records or even scratching, but playing the turntable as a musical instrument in order to produce original and compelling music. At the same time, the foregoing speaks to how shifting perceptions of DJing among my respondents parallels the evolution of DJ culture.

DJ Names, Costs, and Careers

In addition to their entry into DJing, I asked my respondents how they got their DJ names and the significance of those names. In *Black Noise*, Tricia Rose asserts that within the context of African and Afro-diasporic cultural forms in general and hip-hop in particular, "self-naming is a form of reinvention and self-definition."[36] She goes on to state that "rappers, DJs, graffiti artists, and breakdancers all take on hip-hop names and identities that speak to their role, personal characteristics, expertise, or 'claim to fame.'"[37] In the case of hip-hop DJs, they typically take up names that "fuse technology with mastery and style."[38] Given the lack of access of Afro-diasporic youth to conventional means of status formation, these new names and identities provide an alternative and appealing source of status and prestige.[39]

Typically, my respondents culled their DJ names from popular culture, such as video games and films, but they also use variations of their own given names. In many instances, a friend or relative came up with these names. Rygar, for example, got his DJ name from a Nintendo game by the same name, but it is also a combination of the first syllable of his first name (Ryan) and his last name (Garcia), a name given to him by a cousin. In Rygar's view, the fact that his DJ name is based on a popular video game would make it easier for people to remember it.[40] For Rey-Jun, DJ names are simply nicknames, and he does not place much thought and significance in them. He has had several DJ names, and in each case, it was a friend who came up with the name. For my respondents, then, the names they take up are a form of self-definition and self-representation. Similar to the Filipino mobile DJs who came before them, their involvement in DJing allows them to create new identities through the adoption of DJ names and crew affiliations. These names do not necessarily signify mastery of technology but more the individuality and unique styles of my respondents.

As a number of my respondents point out, DJing is an expensive activity to get into, particularly as compared to what it takes to get into the other areas of hip-hop. First and foremost, DJing requires money to buy not only equipment but also records. Statistix, for example, remembers being shocked when he first found out how much a turntable costs.

> STATISTIX: I remember when I asked him, I went into a store I said how much is your intermediate turntable and he said it was about two hundred dollars. I was just blown away. I've never seen two hundred dollars at fourteen years old. But I started all that milk money for lunch, and that's when school started when I eventually bought my very first turntable.[41]

Because of the prohibitive costs of these machines, many of respondents tried to come up with the money themselves instead of relying on their parents. Typically, they could only afford to purchase one piece of equipment at a time rather than the full complement of DJ equipment—one turntable instead of two—or purchase substandard equipment—a Gemini turntable instead of a Technics turntable, which is considered the standard of the field.

The prohibitive costs of DJ equipment, however, did not discourage my respondents from pursuing DJing, including those who self-identify as coming from working-class backgrounds. Celskiii, for example, took a summer job at McDonald's in order to save enough money to buy turntables but also borrowed money from her sister:

> INTERVIEWER: So you were able to save up enough money from just working at McDonald's?
> CELSKIII: Yeah, cause the first set was like, altogether, was probably like four hundred dollars. I worked every weekend when I was in high school and so I would just save hundred dollar checks for about two months. I actually had my sister put it on her credit card and then I had to pay her. But she waited until I gave her two hundred dollars first.
> INTERVIEWER: And you were able to buy all the equipment you needed?
> CELSKIII: Yeah. Before that, I was using my parents' record player, their Sony record player and the tape deck.[42]

The prohibitive costs of DJing also did not stop my respondents from getting into DJing even before they got hold of their own equipment or learned how to operate turntables. Like the Filipino mobile DJs before them, they creatively made use of the available technology or someone else's equipment. A number of my respondents, for instance, messed around with their parents' record player at home or with a friend's turntable.

DJing is not only an expensive activity to get into but also a time-consuming and demanding activity. To become a good DJ means putting in a great deal of hard work to master the fundamentals and nuances of DJing:

> STATISTIX: The only thing about DJing, you just have to have the skills. You just have to know. You can't just wake up in the morning and do it. It takes a lot of practice.[43]
>
> RYGAR: Some people don't understand how hard DJing is, you know. People who say, "Oh mixing, that's easy," but it's actually pretty hard. You gotta put a lot of time into it, a lot of patience.[44]

The DJs I interviewed typically spent countless hours honing their skills, often in isolation in their homes or bedrooms. This was especially the case in preparation for gigs:

> INTERVIEWER: Can you talk a little bit about how much time you spend practicing, like before a gig?
>
> ONE TYME: Once I find out I'm having a gig, I try to practice every day for at least two hours just to listen to my records, know where all my breaks are, like the intros and how a break is, or an intro is, just so like I'm ready. Like, if I don't have a set or lineup, I listen to all the records. I focus on the audience, what kind of crowd is gonna be there, and I pick out the records when I know what they like and the records that they like before that. It's like basically research and just learning from old gigs—like what kind of crowd it is and what kind of music do they like. I just pick out and listen to the intro and breaks. And like, not mixing them but just listening to them to know what record fits well with each other.[45]

DJing, thus, is a time consuming activity that not only involves a lot of practice but also, as One Tyme puts it, "research" in terms of knowing one's audience and what records to play.

Although my respondents do not earn enough from DJing alone to be self-sufficient, it does serve as a valuable source of income, a means to supplement income from their other jobs, and also an appealing alternative to the kind of work generally available to college-age students. Rygar, for example, earns as much as $800 from one night of DJing, which he considers pretty good money and also a much more attractive source of income than a typical nine-to-five job.[46] In Statistix's case, he gravitated toward DJing in part because of the potential to make money, and he earns more from four hours of DJing than a month's work at his other job. He started out earning $200 per gig but he now earns as much as $750 for a night's work.[47]

Beyond the financial rewards that it offers, DJing also provides my respondents with something meaningful to do, an appealing option out of a limited set of alternatives. To illustrate, Celskiii points out that growing up in a working-class family meant growing up in an environment in which her parents were not home a lot, but also growing up in an environment in which there were only a few outlets for recreational activities:

> CELSKIII: Growing in a working-class family, my parents were not home a lot. No one was there. You kind of have to figure out what are you going to do as a kid. You're on your own. . . . After the b-boy scene died, there was a lot of people getting into gangs. Some of my friends got pregnant, and I was thinking, "Okay, I don't fit into any of this." . . . And then there's another group of Filipinos: "Oh hey, we're still going to do hip-hop." And I think that community, that thing kept going that it would put people into it who did not fit into the other crowds, the people who were not gang banging or the people who were not drinking or smoking weed or whatever. People were doing hip-hop still. And then that was something that we did because we did not have parents to take us to ballets you know. You need some kind of simulation when you're younger.[48]

Without parental supervision, the onus was on Celskiii to figure out for herself what to do. While many of her peers became involved in gangs and some of her friends became pregnant, Celskiii gravitated toward hip-hop. For a group of Filipino youth, then, DJing served as an alternative to gangs, the dominant social grouping of the time.

With regard to how DJing figures in these respondents' career plans, some look to DJing as a hobby or a transitional activity and plan to pursue a career unrelated to music. Tease, for instance, majors in marketing, although she admits that she is not very good at it. However, she hopes to use this degree to work in sales in the radio broadcast industry.[49] Statistix considers DJing a significant part of his life, yet he does not envision himself dedicating his life to it. Instead, he plans to become an electrical engineer and looks to DJing more as a vehicle to help him develop social and technical skills he can use in other aspects of his life. In the meantime, however, he hopes to get into the club scene when he turns twenty-one, and he intends to pursue other interests after he finishes college or when he gets married.[50]

In contrast, others look at DJing more as a way of life and plan to pursue careers in music or a field related to music, notwithstanding their college education in fields not related to music. In many ways, this group of respondents is taking advantage of the fact that they got into DJing at a time when career opportunities for DJ have expanded, a time when DJs are no longer limited to spinning at parties or clubs as a means of making a living. Instead, they can support themselves by producing on their own or collaborating with other DJs and MCs. There are also many more avenues for DJs to circulate their music on both a national and international basis.

Celskiii, for example, had planned to pursue a graduate degree and become a college professor. Once she got into DJing, however, she realized that her passion was not school but music:

> INTERVIEWER: So, you know how some people think, "When I start my career," whatever that is, "I'm going to stop DJing." For you, that's clearly not the case.
>
> CELSKIII: I'm going to stop going to school, I was gonna go to grad school right after; like this is my last year, and I was going to go to grad school. But then I was like, "You know, I need to do this." There's a niche and it's something I'm passionate about. I'm more passionate about it than school. And before, I was like, "Oh, ethnic studies." I was really hardcore into learning so much. But then I started to realize, I'm not happy. I started feeling more positive when I started doing music more. It's spiritual too. It gives me energy.[51]

Through DJing, Celskiii has been able to travel and forge social networks on a global scale. She hopes to keep doing music with her DJ partner and collaborator, Deeandroid, and to eventually open their own record store. In addition to DJing, however, Celskiii hopes to work in the community, possibly for a nonprofit. She has already performed at benefits and for nonprofit organizations like the League of Filipino Students (LFS).[52]

Deeandroid's mother is a nurse, and her father is an aircraft mechanic. Likewise, her brother is an aircraft mechanic while her sister attends nursing school. She mentioned that her parents want her to pursue what they consider a stable career like accounting, but Deeandroid has set out to pursue a career in music. For her, what matters more is pursuing something she feels passionate about, even if it means not making a lot of money. Deeandroid considers herself good at business, but she does not plan to pursue it as a career. Instead, she looks at her college education as a secondary option just in case her pursuit of DJing as a career does not pan out.[53]

Rey-Jun's parents want him, along with his older sister, to eventually take over the family business, which comprises four convalescent homes. He feels obligated to do so because, as he puts it, "They built up that business for us, you know, and it's there and they want us to continue it." At this point in his life, however, Rey-Jun considers music more of a priority and a more attractive career option. He did take administrative classes in college, but for the most part, he found them uninteresting. Instead, he hopes to put out music for people to listen and appreciate. For Rey-Jun, being a DJ is a more appealing alternative, because it allows him to be creative and express himself through the production of music, while taking care of the family business is much more mundane and straightforward. Although he does not see it as a potential source of conflict, Rey-Jun has yet to let his parents know how serious he is about pursuing music as a career. He anticipates that his parents will not have a problem with it as long as he manages to earn enough money to survive.[54]

Chapter 4   **"DJing as a Filipino Thing"**
Negotiating Questions of Race

THE DJS I INTERVIEWED ARE WELL AWARE of the history of hip-hop, or what has come to be constructed as the conventional narrative of hip-hop. They are very much aware of the racialized discourses that have come to define the contours of hip-hop, and they acknowledge hip-hop's black antecedents and subscribe to the notion that it began as an African American mode of cultural expression. Yet there is also a sense and recognition among my respondents that the boundaries of hip-hop based on its perceived blackness have been in constant flux. In other words, hip-hop may have started out as a black phenomenon, but it has now evolved into something that encompasses the participation and contributions of multiple groups, including Filipinos.

In this chapter, I delineate the ways Filipino DJs go about framing their engagement with hip-hop and establishing cultural legitimacy given their location outside the foundational narrative of hip-hop. I inquire about the ways my respondents position themselves in relation to hip-hop's purported blackness and their conception of the racial scope of hip-hop. What kinds of authenticating claims do they make, and what kinds of authenticating strategies do they rely on? How do Filipino youth position themselves in relation to hip-hop's hierarchy of authenticity, which places a premium on exhibiting signifiers of blackness? On what basis do they generate their own signifiers of authenticity and claim hip-hop as their own? How does blackness figure in their conception of hip-hop? If they no longer conceive of hip-hop as an African American expressive form, then how do they view it? On what basis? How do they conceive of the relationship between Filipinoness and hip-hop? More broadly, I am interested in how my respondents approach questions of race, culture, and authenticity.

The DJs I interviewed carve out a niche within hip-hop by attempting to establish cultural legitimacy and belongingness in terms other than proximity to blackness. They do so by relying on a variety of authenticating strategies, strategies that range from efforts to foreground lived experience as the basis of their involvement in hip-hop to efforts to foreground hip-hop's transcendent appeal. In making these authenticating claims, my respondents attempt to present their own narrative of hip-hop that is compatible with the standard narrative, but they also claim a different kind of authenticity for themselves that is not in any way imitative or a derivative of blackness. Filipino youth participation in hip-hop, therefore, can be read as one of intense cultural negotiation with the perceived racial scope of hip-hop and authenticating claims based on its purported blackness, which has implications for the way Filipino youth stake out their position and presence in U.S. society.

Authenticating Strategies of Filipino DJs

Filipino DJs in particular and Filipino American youth in general are not in a position to make originary and historical claims as the basis of their cultural entitlement and authenticity. Unlike Puerto Rican youth, for example, Filipino youth were not among the first MCs, DJs, writers, and b-boys/b-girls, which could have buttressed their claims of cultural belongingness. In addition, Filipino and black youth do not have a sense of shared history and culture, at least not to the same extent that exists between Puerto Ricans and blacks in a place like New York, where the two groups have overlapping experiences of racialization, marginalization, and labor exploitation. Puerto Ricans and African Americans also have parallel cultural traditions and practices to the extent that both have served as precursors to the emergence of hip-hop. And unlike Puerto Rican youth, Filipino youth cannot claim blackness or an African/diasporic racial identity.

So while hip-hop constitutes an important realm of interaction, collaboration, and conflict between Puerto Rican youth and black youth, it does not constitute the same kind of space for Filipino youth and black youth. This is not to deny that at times Puerto Ricans have challenged their racialization as black in the United States or instances when hip-hop does serve as an important realm of cross-racial interaction between Filipino and black youth, but more to account for the specificities of Filipino and Puerto Rican youth and to recognize that Filipino involvement in hip-hop is not easily mapped onto the critical frames that hip-hop scholars like Tricia Rose, Juan Flores, and Raquel Z. Rivera deploy for black and Puerto Rican youth respectively.[1]

The incommensurability of Filipino presence in hip-hop with the Puerto Rican presence—what Ian Maxwell has described as "the absence of a cultural, ethnic, geographical, or historical continuity with the origins of hip-hop"[2]—

means that Filipino youth cannot rely on the same set of legitimizing discourses and claims, and thus they have to advance a very different set of discourses and claims and deploy other strategies to bolster them. It means that Filipino youth rely on authenticating strategies that echo the strategies of other groups, but while parallels can be drawn between the authenticating strategies of other non–African American youth and Filipino DJs, it is important not to lose sight of the specificities of Filipino youth involvement in DJing.

Foregrounding Lived Experience

One of the ways my respondents attempt to establish and enhance their cultural legitimacy is by foregrounding lived experience as the basis for their involvement in hip-hop, deploying what E. Patrick Johnson terms in another context as "experience narratives."[3] In other words, they authenticate their involvement in DJing by narrativizing their experiences of growing up with and embracing hip-hop at an early age. I asked my respondents, for example, if they consider hip-hop part of Filipino culture, and a number of them responded affirmatively:

> DEEANDROID: Yeah, I think it's part of Filipino culture, because it's what the generation—that's what we're doing here and we're Filipinos. And you know, hip-hop is part of growing up. And so yeah, it's definitely part of being in the Filipino culture because it's there. It's around you.[4]
>
> CELSKIII: And plus, I mean I know where it came from and who put it out, but then growing up in Vallejo, Filipinos were doing it, and that's what I grew up with. So I was not feeling like we're doing a black thing. It is a Filipino thing, and even my uncles when I was four who just came from the Philippines, they were breakdancing in the garage. And I remember that, I remember that from long time ago, seeing it around my neighborhood and in my family.[5]
>
> RYGAR: That's what mostly Filipinos are into. That's just the way, it's just part of us now, 'cause I mean, generations and generations will come; it's just going to go bigger to the point where . . . I don't even know; it's just part of us already. No one can deny it . . . I would have to say that DJing cause yeah, whenever people look at Filipinos I'm pretty sure they think of DJing, DJs you know.[6]

In the excerpt above, Celskiii pays homage to the acknowledged originators of hip-hop, but at the same time, she makes it clear that she never felt like she was engaging in an African American expressive form. Rygar speaks more specifically about DJing but expresses similar sentiments, alluding to how DJing has become synonymous with Filipinoness by virtue of the fact that "that's what Filipinos are into." Anticipating the intergenerational transmission of hip-hop culture among Filipinos, Rygar, makes the claim that DJing is a "part of us already."

For my respondents, then, hip-hop constitutes an expressive form they are more intimately familiar with than the culture of their parents, an expressive form they consider no less authentically "Filipino" than practices tradition-ally associated with Filipinoness. This speaks to the way DJing has come to serve as a rite of passage among Filipino youth and interwoven into their everyday lives. Rivera makes a similar point in relation to Puerto Rican youth involvement in hip-hop: "Furthermore, hip-hop is as vernacular (or "native") to a great many New York Puerto Ricans as the culture of their parents and grandparents."[7] They may not have been there from the start, but for my respondents, hip-hop is as much a part of their lives as forms and practices commonly identified as Filipino, a widespread practice among those they grew up with—peers, relatives, and older siblings who were already immersed in an aspect of hip-hop culture.

In this kind of strategy, my respondents claim cultural legitimacy on the basis of a particular kind of experience, a function of growing up in the Bay Area with its rich history of Filipino youth involvement in hip-hop rather than shared experiences with African Americans. They point to their immer-sion in hip-hop culture without seemingly making a conscious and concerted effort to do so, an authenticating strategy that lends their engagement with hip-hop an "organic" quality (as opposed, for example, to their getting involved because of media influence or exposure). In short, my respondents are sim-ply being true to their lived experiences.

In claiming hip-hop as their own, my respondents are subscribing to a particular view of culture that Flores describes: "Culture as a source of iden-tity does need to be understood as a flexible, open-ended process grounded in lived experience; but it is also a process in the sense that it is constituted."[8] In the view of my respondents, they are not simply adopting black cultural forms and practices but engaging in creative rearticulations of these forms and practices in a way that resonates with their own experiences. Culture in this sense is not simply a matter of heritage to be passed on from one generation to the next but negotiated on a daily basis. This is especially the case in the realm of DJing, which has become an important source of pride and cultural legit-imation among my respondents in particular, and Filipino youth in general.

Being True to the Principles or Values of Hip-hop

Another way my respondents attempt to stake out their cultural legitimacy is by emphasizing that Filipino youth have been true to the principles or values of hip-hop. In many ways, this strategy echoes the statement that appears in the Mountain Brothers' publicity packet in which group members, primarily Chinese Americans, express their "dedication to the art":

> Because of [the Mountain Brother's] dedication to the art, they (like the origi-nators and true keepers of hip-hop) bring the kind of material that will add to hip-hop music, not steal from it or cheapen it. No shallow gimmicks, no karate kicks, no horror movie blood splattering, no "songs that sound like the group that went platinum," just straight up self truth. What the Mountain Brothers represent most of all is a deep love, respect, and ability for true "rewind the shit over and over in your walkman" hip-hop.[9]

Several of the DJs I interviewed likewise emphasize their "love" and "respect" for the culture and commitment to what they perceive as the true essence of hip-hop.

> SOUP-A-CRUNK: I think it does matter. I think it's a good thing mainly because it's a part of hip-hop and we have a firm hold on it. But really, Filipinos repre-sent in all aspects. It's a matter of recognition. I mean, it's not like we're look-ing for recognition, 'cause we're gonna be in it whether or not we do. It's just that we're in it because we love it. I think it's important because it shows how diverse it is, how hip-hop is, and it represents—how it is for the people.[10]

In Soup-a-Crunk's view, it is this emotional attachment to and investment in hip-hop that not only legitimizes Filipino participation in hip-hop but also makes it possible to transcend racial difference. Their "dedication to the art" allows Filipinos to align themselves with "the originators and true keepers of hip-hop," affording them cultural authenticity.

In this context, the notion of "represent" means a commitment to pre-serving the integrity of hip-hop and elevating the culture, which takes on added significance given the corporate takeover of hip-hop and subsequent pronouncements of its demise. Soup-a-Crunk relies on what Shuhei Hoso-kawa describes in another context as "rhetoric of an affective connection that makes the particular appeal of a musical style universally relevant."[11] This rhetoric usually takes the form of "respect" and "passion" (or in Soup-a-Crunk's case, "love") for the culture, which has the effect of universalizing hip-hop. In other words, assertions of belongingness are made on the basis of affective claims that allow anyone to establish cultural legitimacy and become part of a broader community that transcends history, geography, culture, and race. In effect, affective grounds for claiming hip-hop trumps the location of Filipino youth outside the foundational narrative of hip-hop.

Z-Trip invokes a similar kind of logic as a way to reconnect with a particular era in hip-hop history, what he describes as early hip-hop, which is in keeping with the valorization of the old school and what it signifies:[12]

> As turntablists we were trying to make the instrument of the turntable do things it's not supposed to. We developed our own decks, mixers, tone arms, needles, everything we needed to facilitate experimentation. We took the baton from the early hip-hop and house DJs and ran with it. Pushing the craft of DJing to new levels was the main thing for us—the only thing. DJs now are so worried about getting to the big paychecks, but we were just focusing on the music.[13]

By the same token, then, my respondents are invoking a particular tradition exemplified by Z-Trip's invocation of "early hip-hop," a discursive maneuver that not only romanticizes hip-hop "back in the day" but also positions turntablists as the true heirs and embodiment of hip-hop values and principles.

Pointing to Hip-hop's Transcendent Appeal

Another way my respondents attempt to stake out their cultural legitimacy is by pointing to hip-hop's transcendent appeal even as they acknowledge its black antecedents. Soup-a-Crunk, for example, refers to hip-hop as a "human thing" and invokes the signifier "the people." In doing so, Soup-a-Crunk is appealing to what Hans Weisethaunet and Ulf Lindberg refer to as the "folk-loric version of 'authenticity,'"[14] the notion of music (in this case hip-hop) as somehow signifying the sentiments and values of the people:

> SOUP-A-CRUNK: Definitely. I mean it originated from them folks. I mean originally it was a way to keep people out of violence with Afrika Bambaataa. It was a way to speak to the fellows and bring them up and keep them from violence. But then really, it's more of like, it's not just a racial thing; it's kind of like a human thing that spoke to the people rather than just a specific race, you know. That's why so many people feel it—it's because it comes down to human qualities.[15]

One Tyme refers to hip-hop as a "worldwide thing" that brings together people of "different ethnicities." This is particularly the case in the hip-hop underground scene:

> ONE TYME: I think television, it's all the media, 'cause that's all they show. They don't go to these underground shows where it's total diverse groups, like you see a lot of Latin Americans or Filipino Americans or African Americans, white Americans. They're just, like, all there peacefully watching a concert. But I think the media plays a big role. They just show, like, the money and, like, the fights and everything bad that goes down. But they don't see all these different ethnicities coming together at a party just having fun. So I think hip-hop, turntablism is

worldwide thing, which a lot of people don't know. Like, they've it in Germany, it's really big in Japan, and, like, the UK, and people don't know that. They need to be more aware of that.[16]

For both Soup-a-Crunk and One Tyme, no one group has a sole proprietary claim on hip-hop, and they question the notion that ethnic and racial affiliation has a direct bearing on questions of cultural belonging and entitlement. Hip-hop, in other words, operates as a purely transcendental signifier with no simple or straightforward referent.

In effect, Soup-a-Crunk and One Tyme subscribe to what David Hesmondhalgh and Caspar Melville describe as a "utopian discourse of collectivism and equality" predicated on "the breaking down of ethnic, class, and gender differences."[17] The authors in this instance are referencing the construction of club culture in Britain as a democratizing force as evidenced by slogans such as "No performers, no VIPS, we are all special."[18] For Soup-a-Crunk and One Tyme, then, hip-hop signifies a utopic space of togetherness and inclusion, a kind of populism that has been associated with dance culture. A similar kind of discourse operates within the house music scene in which the club serves as a utopic space. As Brian Currid puts it: "The effects of raced power as they operate 'within' this community are erased, as all the dancers of the club, dancing (coincidentally) to a black musical form, enact their 'togetherness,' without any consciousness of race, class, or gender difference; in the darkness of the club, the social significances of skin color disappear."[19]

DJing, Filipinoness, and U.S. Racial Formations

Viewed within the context of Filipino invisibility, DJing constitutes an important mode of self-representation, allowing Filipino youth to negotiate the terms of their racialization and render their experience meaningful and intelligible. It becomes a way for Filipino youth to assume their own distinct identity in contradistinction to the racialization of hip-hop as black and their own categorization as Asian American. This is the backdrop against which Filipino youth define and understand their Filipinoness as well as locate and differentiate themselves within contemporary racial formations. In doing so, they demonstrate that the production of Filipinoness is not done in isolation but in relation to racialized discourses and practices in the United States.

DJing confers upon Filipino youth a collective status and public visibility, a status and visibility denied to them through the conventional channels of the dominant culture, such as school and the media, which generally overlook the experiences of Filipinos. The failure of these institutions to engage with the realities of Filipinos in the United States has compelled Filipino youth to look elsewhere for meaningful forms of expression and identification, relying on a more accessible and appealing medium to counteract the low symbolic capital associated with Filipinoness. The turn to DJing, therefore, can be understood as a way for Filipino youth to carve out a space of their own and assert their ethnic/racial identity within the U.S. racial imaginary.

For many of my respondents, DJing has become an important source for the validation and recognition of Filipinoness, a vehicle for the consolidation of cultural capital. Rey-Jun had the following to say about the significance of DJing to Filipino youth in answering the question of whether DJing gives Filipinos a name not just within hip-hop but also within the broader U.S. social and cultural landscape:

> REY-JUN: I would think so, especially in California and the East Coast because at least for a decade, Filipinos were the top DJs, the top battle DJs in the world. Yeah it would because without it, a lot of people would not know who Filipinos are in terms of the hip-hop community, in terms of people in the East Coast, in terms of people throughout the country. DJing really gave us an identity. DJing has given Filipinos a name, especially in the hip-hop community. I mean, when I started out DJing, Q-Bert was the best DJ out there.[20]

As Filipinos have come to be acknowledged as the best DJs in the world, so DJing has afforded Filipino youth the opportunity to forge a culture and develop a style they could call their own and, at the same time, get the recognition Rey-Jun believes Filipino youth have earned. DJing has provided them with a cultural space they can claim as their domain, contributing to a sense of group pride and belonging.

By the same token, DJing enables Filipino youth to contest the terms by which Filipinos are racialized in the United States and to assert the specificities of their Filipinoness. Following Elizabeth H. Pisares, it is a way for Filipino youth to counteract the racial ambiguity that has come to surround Filipinos in the United States as a function of their postwar racialization. The popular Pinay dance music artist Jocelyn Enriquez, for example, suggests that the classification of Filipinos as Asian American has proven to be consequential in terms of contributing to a sense of being lost: "Because you know, being Filipino we get lost, people don't really know what Filipinos are. If you're Asian, you're either going to be Japanese or Chinese."[21]

Enriquez's comments resonate with a number of my respondents, who spoke of the misrecognition that seems to plague Filipinos in the United States.

One Tyme, for example, had the following to say about the absence of Filipino public figures in the United States:

> INTERVIEWER: I guess it's hard to think of someone else.
> ONE TYME: Yeah it really is. There's other people they say, "Oh, she's Filipino." I'm like, "Really?" It's like they can't tell that they're Filipino or confused into Asian Americans or like Chinese Americans. It's like we don't have our own identity, like Filipino thing. It's like, you don't know who's Filipino who's not.[22]

Onetyme herself has not been immune from this kind of misrecognition, as she initially thought that Q-Bert was Chinese because of his light skin. Likewise, her comments speak to the absence of reliable markers of Filipinoness.

Among my respondents, then, there is acknowledgment of the lack of recognition that surrounds the presence of Filipinos in the United States. For Rey-Jun, this stems from the classification of Filipinos as Asian American, which, in his view, constitutes a form of erasure, and he provides an analysis of why he claims for himself a Filipino identity:

> INTERVIEWER: You mentioned earlier how Filipinos are not really Asians. Could you talk a little bit more about why you don't identify yourself as Asian even though a lot of people lump Filipinos with Asian.
> REY-JUN: Because it's so broad it does not give us an identity. Compared to Asians, Filipinos are different. We're influenced by Spanish. They lump us with Asians because of region, not culture.[23]

In Rey-Jun's view, region, or geography, serves as a problematic basis for categorizing Filipinos as Asian American because of the way it elides the particularities of Filipinos and their historical placement within U.S. society. Instead, he considers "Filipino" a cultural term, looking to culture as a more meaningful basis of categorization, although he does not elaborate on the broader implications.[24]

Rey-Jun's comments demonstrate a self-awareness of his own racialization and that of Filipinos as "Asian American" in contemporary U.S. society as well as the vexed and contentious relationship of Filipinos to Asian American panethnic formations. They speak to how Filipino self-identification is at odds with U.S. racial formations but also to how Filipinos have negotiated the terms of their racialization. Furthermore, his comments shed light on the need to conceptualize Filipinoness in much broader and historical terms, in a way that accounts for the singularity or exceptionality of Filipinos in relation to other Asian American groups. And in pointing to culture as a possibly more meaningful basis of categorization, Rey-Jun gestures toward alternative modes of identification that are better suited to speak to the specificities of Filipinos so that they would not be seen, in Pisares's words, "as everything and anything but Filipino."[25]

More to the point, the categorization of Filipinos as Asian American not only distorts the specificities of Filipinos but also the possibility of other modes of group identification that is encompassing of shared histories between Filipinos and other groups. Filipinos may indeed share some affinities with other Asian American groups, but in other, more substantive ways, they also belong among other groups. Because of their colonial history, for example, Filipinos could just as easily be grouped with such groups as Chicanos, Puerto Ricans, Native Americans, and Pacific Islanders. Yet the subsumption of Filipinos within the Asian American category obfuscates these shared experiences of colonization, conquest, and displacement, as Filipinoness is seen as categorically distinct from, rather than partially overlapping with these categories. It occludes how Filipinos are linked as much with these groups as with any Asian American group they are generally grouped with in popular accounts.[26]

Within the context of Filipino invisibility, then, Filipinos look to culture as a vehicle to assert and narrate their presence on their own terms. In other words, culture serves as an important marker through which Filipino youth negotiate with the absence of a Filipino American racial discourse. As Pisares suggests, they do so in multiple ways, including identification as Asian American, the construction of a racial discourse around the notion of brownness, and the fetishization of ethnic markers as evident in culture shows. She goes on to point out that DJing provides an alternative to these modes of Filipino American identity and cultural formation, an alternative that does not run into the same kinds of complications.[27]

In the case of ISP, Pisares makes the point that rather than assert their Filipinoness through their music, the group engages in a strategic refusal to racialize their involvement in DJing. Instead, their aim is to innovate and perfect the techniques associated with this expressive form, as evidenced by the following quote from Q-Bert: "We're not Filipino artists, we're artists. We're not from the Filipino race, we're from the human race. . . . Ever since we started, race didn't matter to us. As soon as it does matter, there's something wrong. It never occurred to us that being Filipinos would hinder us in doing what we love. It never crossed out minds. What crossed our minds is we have to practice. That's what would hinder us."[28] Pisares goes on to argue that it is precisely because ISP is not bound to a racially defined musical genre or obligated to create music identifiably Filipino that allows them to excel in an art form like DJing to the point where no one can ignore a Filipino presence. In other words, Filipino invisibility has actually opened up a space for Filipino youth to excel in an expressive form like DJing.[29]

Q-Bert and Post-Race Discourse

The example of Q-Bert is particularly instructive in this regard because of the way he positions himself in relation to discourses surrounding his Filipino-ness and what this reveals about the contours of contemporary discourses on race. More specifically, an interrogation of his iconicity reveals the convergence of multiple discourses, including those of American individualism, colorblindness, liberal pluralism, and meritocracy. On more than one occasion, for example, Q-Bert has invoked the notion of "human race" to describe the relevance of his music: "I feel like whatever I do is pretty much not just for the Filipino community. It's for everyone. Real music should be appreciated by anyone, and I'm more on the universal tip as far as the Filipino pride stuff. We're all the same race, the human race."[30] In his self-presentation, then, Q-Bert downplays race as an issue. Instead, he looks to DJing as a race neutral activity, frequently positioning himself as a DJ who just happens to be Filipino. Yet for my respondents and Filipino youth at large, Q-Bert constitutes a potent symbol of Filipinoness precisely because of his ethnic background despite a concerted effort on his part to downplay his Filipinoness or be seen as an "ethnic" artist.

For Pisares, this kind of discourse is in many ways a function of what she characterizes as the "perceptual absence" or "racial ambiguity" that plagues Filipinos in the United States. In her view, DJing constitutes a distinct mode of self-representation conditioned by the exclusion of Filipinos from racial discourse, a mode of self-representation marked by a distinctive kind of discourse and self-narration. As Pisares herself acknowledges, however, DJing may very well represent an advance over other modes of Filipino American representation, but it is not without complications. For one thing, "the abstract character of music that otherwise lends itself to the creativity of those listening from outside racial discourse impedes the ability of Filipino Americans to confront their invisibility via the turntable (though their massive success has made issues about Filipino American participation in hip-hop unavoidable). Indeed, some of the premier Filipino American DJs are adamant about the meritocratic nature of turntablism: hard work and not identity, they argue, makes a battle champ."[31] Pisares also comments on efforts by Filipino American DJs at self-narration, efforts that are generally oriented toward the future and outer space in contrast to that of African Americans:

African American DJs easily connect their craft with a history-laden sense of time and place, invoking hip-hop's origins in South Bronx housing projects, as a response to racial segregation, gang violence and urban decay. In contrast, Filipino American DJs asked to identify their music's origins and influences speak of future time and outer space. While space ships, eight-armed extraterrestrials, and other figments of science fiction serve as what Oliver Wang calls a "Filipino-futurism," an alternative discourse that compensates for the absence of race, it is not as if Filipino Americans did not have their own neighborhoods, institutions, and social practices amidst racial isolation and hierarchy.[32]

But in resorting to discourses of meritocracy and "Filipino-futurism," Filipino DJs also risk reproducing the logic informing contemporary discourses about diversity, difference, and race in the United States.

Similarly, Juliana Snapper asserts that Q-Bert and other Filipino turntablists may very well be engaging in racially subversive practices in relation to the prevailing logic of U.S. racial discourse. They engage in what Snapper describes as "performative ambiguity" that speaks to the potential of turntablism to trouble existing racial categories and logic. She notes, for example, how turntablists, including Filipino turntablists, are difficult to locate racially: "A listener's preconceived race/nation assumptions fail as often as not, creating a zone of racial uncertainty."[33] In effect, Filipino DJs are partaking in practices that could be described as anti-essentialist because of their refusal to let their Filipinoness overdetermine the music they produce.

In distancing himself from his status as a racialized subject, Q-Bert is reverting to a practice common among artists of color: that of disavowing their ethnic and racial background as way to negotiate with expectations to represent the "race" or in this case, Filipinos as a group. But in viewing his popularity within a deracinated context, Q-Bert, in effect, is resorting to the reactionary, color-blind discourse that has become the sine qua non of contemporary popular cultural politics. Accordingly, he makes it seem as if his popularity can be reduced to his outstanding DJ skills rather than taking place within a particular set of circumstances in which his Filipinoness plays a prominent role. This kind of disavowal, then, functions to displace issues of race and power, rendering questions of social and cultural identity benign.

Contemporary Filipino Youth Cultural Politics

In many ways, the DJs I interviewed articulate a kind of cultural politics that resonates with the cultural politics of Q-Bert. One could argue that in conceiving of hip-hop as a "human thing" or a "worldwide thing," my respondents risk reproducing the very logic of a liberal pluralist view of diversity.

This deracialized account of hip-hop is problematic because it effaces the particular set of circumstances out of which hip-hop emerged—the racialized and political specificity of hip-hop that accounts for much of its potential as a transformative force. For a number of my respondents, to acknowledge race or conceive of hip-hop in race-conscious terms would seemingly compromise their authenticating claims and legitimacy.

Moreover, reading hip-hop within this framework obscures how different groups of youth are racialized in different ways that, in turn, condition the manner in which they negotiate with the racialized discourses and authenticating claims circulating within hip-hop. It fails to illuminate the field of racial positions within hip-hop and the power asymmetries that underwrite these positions. Likewise, this kind of reading overlooks how culture is differently or differentially experienced and contested within and between groups of youth.[34] To borrow from Anita Mannur, this sort of reading divests expressive forms (in this case hip-hop) "of any racialized or classed implications."[35] In other words, a level of equivalence is assumed in which difference is acknowledged only to be reconfigured as part of a colorful mosaic that is hip-hop.

The reading of hip-hop as a transcendent space is a familiar argument but is also symptomatic of the ways the discourse of race works in the United States, as well as the ways this understanding of race informs contemporary articulations of Filipinoness. It can be seen as an instance of a broader discourse about race, culture, and difference that overlooks the ways racialization has played out differently for various groups. The tendency is to shy away from overt identity claims (particularly along the lines of race) and instead to resort to claims of liberal pluralism in which "difference" is rendered benign and safe for consumption in the marketplace and elaborated in nonracial or cultural terms—what Virginia R. Dominguez has called in another context as the "culturalization of difference."[36] According to this formulation, then, Filipinoness becomes just another marker of difference, "a kind of difference that does not make a difference of any kind,"[37] overlooking the social, economic, and historical contexts surrounding the racialization of Filipinos in the United States.

My respondents may very well be subscribing to a discourse symptomatic of what Dylan Rodriguez has termed "Filipino Americanism" that seeks, in his words, "(1) *civil recognition* as a viable and self-contained collective subject of the U.S. polity (including and beyond nomination as 'citizens' of the nation), and (2) *cultural valorization* as cooperative and richly contributing to the historical telos of American nation building in the post–civil rights, multiculturalist moment."[38] Crucial to Rodriguez's formulation and especially relevant to my study is his consideration of Filipino American cultural productions as a constituent element of an emergent Filipino American common sense. He provides a reading of Q-Bert's iconicity very much in line with my own reading, specifically taking issue with Q-Bert's color-blind discourse that echoes a strain of what Rodriguez describes as "Filipino American common sense, which attempts to locate the putative Filipino body, genealogy, and historical condition beyond the parochialisms of racial classification, such that 'the Filipino' is sometimes positioned outside raciality altogether."[39] Following Rodriguez, my respondents may very well be embracing the same logic that "enable[s] the relations of dominance integral to U.S. social formation."[40]

In other ways, however, my respondents articulate a kind of racial politics that represents a marked departure from Q-Bert's liberal pluralism. To illustrate, not all my respondents interpret the broadening ethno-racial scope of hip-hop in the same way. In the following, Celskiii and Rey-Jun provide an important counterpoint to the reading of hip-hop as a transcendent space, recognizing that the evolution of hip-hop from a "black thing" to a global phenomenon has been far from seamless and unproblematic. For them, the cross-cultural appeal of hip-hop is inextricably bound up to its commercial appeal, but it has also meant a depoliticization of its black antecedents and continued black influence as reflected in the changing face of hip-hop audiences and in the changing influences of hip-hop:

CELSKIII: It's like people in hip-hop, there's not even a lot of people who are black anymore. When you go to hip-hop shows, it's all white. There's not even Filipinos. I don't even see Filipinos anymore. . . . I'm aware of, there's a problem in hip-hop right now. Why aren't there a lot of black people? Why are there a lot of white people? But I also know it became more universal to people when it became commercial or commodified.[41]

INTERVIEWER: Do you consider it part of black culture?

REY-JUN: Yeah I do. I really did not look at it as part of black culture back then. I just thought of it as music. But then now that I look back, it definitely was. Back in the day, native tongues and all that stuff, everyone was trying to be black. It had a major influence on society. It did. If you're into hip-hop, you got influenced by black culture, because that's how powerful it was then.

INTERVIEWER: You still look at like that today?

REY-JUN: I do, but it's not like that at all. With the underground it is, but today, I would say about fifty percent of rappers, it's all about making money. Back in the day, we were influenced by black culture; today, they're influenced by the money and sex and all that because that's all you hear on the radio these days. You really need to know where it came from or grew up in that era to, like, really find out the basis of real hip-hop music is.[42]

Celskiii's and Rey-Jun's comments demonstrate a politicized understanding of the ways in which blackness is not simply a signifier of what is considered "hip" or "cool" but also a site of political identification and contestation. In Celskiii's case, she points out that underlying the universalization of hip-hop is its mass commodification while in Rey-Jun's case, he points out that the depoliticization of hip-hop is inextricably linked to its mass commodification.

Conclusion

In problematizing the claims of my respondents and the underlying basis for their claims, I do not mean to argue that hip-hop is the absolute or specific cultural property of African Americans because they created it, or to argue that the participation of nonblack practitioners and participants have brought about a "dilution" of hip-hop as a function of their purported distance from hip-hop's point of origin. Rather, my goal is to argue for a much more complex understanding of culture, one that takes into account the tensions and ambiguities inherent in the traversing of cultural boundaries. It is to argue for the need to interrogate what it means to deploy the signifier "black" in relation to hip-hop today, given hip-hop's diffusion on a global scale. I am particularly interested in the question of what it means to account for the global diffusion of hip-hop without losing sight of its "black" origins and continued "black" influence. How do we hold these two in a productive tension? What does the appeal to "roots" and "origins" signify in this context and to what effect? Does an appeal to roots and origins render illegitimate any forms and practices that do not emerge from the original context of hip-hop? Are all appeals to roots and origins necessarily suspect? What is obscured by the impossibility or irrelevance of origins? What are the politics at stake?[43]

The tendency, particularly with regard to black expressive forms and practices, is to conceive of the kinds of intercultural exchanges that take place as an issue simply of appropriation or a cultural "free-for-all." In other words, black culture is conceived simply as something to be plundered, or a level of equivalence is assumed among the different groups of youth participating. In either case, black culture is located outside history and disentangled from politics. Overlooked are the specificities of the groups in question—their status and positionality—as well as the ways culture remains linked to race despite efforts to obscure this connection.

Chapter 5 The Normative Boundaries of Filipinoness

> It's just, just being in the spotlight is fun, you know. 'Cause when you're a DJ at a party, you're the party, you know. You're the one that controls the mood, you're the one that controls what people say, you know. Like, uh, you can say anything to the crowd. Like, if you're doing good, you can manipulate the crowd to make them do whatever you want. I've had that at frat parties—just hella crazy.
>
> —Rygar

> I notice that when we're spinning, we get these second glances. It's irritating but it's kind of like they don't expect us to play good music. They expect us to play—I don't know. I guess it's hard for some of them to think of women having good taste in music or having knowledge of music. When we scratch, it's always like, "Oh shit, girl."
>
> —Celskiii

IN CLAIMING HIP-HOP AS THEIR OWN, the DJs I interviewed are engaging in a practice that is not completely new. Instead, these DJs are building on a tradition when they look to new cultural options and alternatives and claim as their own an expressive form not considered Filipino in a way that speaks to their specific circumstances and concerns. At the same time, they bring attention to the complex subject positions and shifting identifications of Filipinos from one era to another and from generation to generation, but also the contested and ambivalent nature of this process. They raise questions over what is considered the legitimate boundaries of Filipinoness, the terms by which these boundaries are understood, and to what effects. More broadly, DJing constitutes a means for simultaneously negotiating the terms by which the Filipino diaspora has been narrativized.

As evidenced by what Rygar and Celskiii say, however, Filipino youth involvement in DJ culture constitutes a highly gendered stratified space with different implications for Pinoy DJs and Pinay DJ in terms of their experiences and the way they negotiate their place within the culture. It is shaped not only by gendered expectations particular to DJ culture but also by expectations grounded in normative notions of Filipino manhood and womanhood that further serve to delimit Pinay youth participation in DJing. DJ culture constitutes a male domain in which female DJs occupy a subordinate position within the power and status hierarchy of DJ culture. At the same time, Filipino parents generally view their daughters' participation in DJing as a transgression of the boundaries of Filipinaness, in contrast to their sons' pursuit of DJing, which is seen as compatible with normative notions of Filipinoness. It is within this context that Pinoy and Pinay DJs attempt to carve out their place within DJing and, in the process of doing so, adopt but also confound established meanings of masculinity and femininity circulating within DJ culture and deployed in the diaspora.

In this chapter, then, I delineate the ways my respondents turn to DJing to reconstitute what it means to be Filipino. For Pinoy youth, DJing affords them an opportunity to accumulate a good deal of status and prestige.[1] It makes possible the production and performance of an emergent Filipino masculinity built around the mastery of technical and musical skills. For Pinay youth, however, DJing has not afforded them the same kind of opportunity or provided the same kind of space. Instead, Pinay youth engage in a number of different strategies to negotiate with and challenge the normative boundaries of DJ culture and Filipinoness particularly along gender lines.

Reconfiguring the Boundaries of Filipinoness within the Context of the Diaspora

In my interviews with Filipino DJs, it became apparent that they do not adhere to authentic notions of "tradition" or "culture" or look to conventional markers of Filipinoness such as language, food, and religion to construct their sense of Filipinoness. By the same token, they do not feel culturally inauthentic because of having been born and raised in the United States. This is not to suggest that my respondents completely dissociate themselves from practices and traditions considered "Filipino." A number of my respondents, for example, expressed a desire to someday visit the Philippines. Instead, it is to suggest that for them, those practices and traditions considered Filipino are what Yen Le Espiritu has described as cursory manifestations of culture that are "periodic and thus have little or no relevance to their daily life."[2]

In considering DJing to be as much a Filipino thing as cultural forms and practices considered Filipino, my respondents are subscribing to a view of cultural identity not predicated on the reification of the homeland as the originary and authentic source of Filipinoness, as in the case of culture shows such as Pilipino Cultural Night (PCN).[3] For them, cultural affiliation is not just about identification with the cultural heritage of their parents or adoption of cultural practices passed on from generation to generation but a much more dynamic process that is grounded in specific historical contexts and changes over time. To borrow from Stuart Hall, cultural identity from this perspective "is a matter of 'becoming' as well as 'being.' It belongs to the future as much as to the past. It is not something which already exists, transcending place, time, history and culture."[4]

One can argue that my respondents are not evincing a diasporic identity and consciousness precisely because they do not look to the Philippines as the exclusive or primary source of Filipinoness. The turn to black sources and traditions, then, can be perceived as representing a "loss of culture" or a "loss of tradition," a threat to the cultural integrity and stability of the category "Filipino." This line of thinking, however, assumes that formations rooted in the Philippines are authentic, while formations rooted elsewhere in the diaspora are inauthentic or less authentic. It assumes that "Filipino culture" can be reduced to one set of traditions one can turn to at the "appropriate" moment to get in touch with their Filipinoness rather than a dynamic set of social relations contingent on context, history, place, and space. In effect, diaspora remains "the bastard child of the nation—disavowed, inauthentic, illegitimate, an impoverished imitation of the originary culture."[5]

The turn to DJing as a source of Filipinoness, however, can also be understood as symptomatic of the need to expand the frame within which the contours of Filipinoness have historically been defined. It is symptomatic of the need to consider how Filipinoness is transformed and reconstructed in the diaspora, referencing not only formations "back home" but also formations in a variety of diasporic contexts. To borrow from Paul Gilroy, the "critical space/time cartography of the diaspora needs therefore to be readjusted so that the dynamics of dispersal and local autonomy can be shown alongside the unforeseen detours and circuits which mark the new journeys and new arrivals that, in turn, release new political and cultural possibilities."[6]

Building on Gilroy's insight, it is no longer adequate to continue to privilege the homeland as the singular originary site of Filipinoness, or to conceive of the spatial and temporal cartography of the Filipino diaspora in linear terms, because to do so obscures the varied and changing expressions of Filipinoness. Accordingly, the Philippines constitutes just another location in the Filipino diasporic circuit, just as "Filipino" cultural practices and traditions constitute just one element that goes into the production of Filipino identity and culture. Similarly, the production and maintenance of "culture" is not just a matter of cultural inheritance or nostalgia for an idealized homeland but a much more selective and creative process referencing elements of various cultural sources and traditions, including those not considered Filipino. The Filipino diaspora, therefore, should be seen not as reflecting a singular sense of identification but as constituting a space for multiple identifications, with the Philippines constituting one mode in this global circuit.

Rather than signifying a "loss of culture" or a "loss of tradition," then, the turn to DJing could be seen as signifying a reworking of culture and tradition by Filipino youth in an attempt to redefine for themselves what it means to be Filipino at this contemporary moment as well as make culture relevant and meaningful. In other words, it can no longer be assumed that nostalgia, longing, and loss are *the* central themes that define the contours of Filipino diasporic subjectivities and experiences, or that they exhaust the kinds of identification available to Filipino youth. Instead, Filipino youth involvement in DJing serves to reconfigure the normative boundaries of Filipinoness predicated on nostalgia and the (re)production of cultural linkages with an idealized homeland. It opens up alternative ways of thinking about Filipinoness—U.S. or diaspora based rather than Philippine or homeland based—that speak to the complex social locations and shifting identifications of Filipinos in the diaspora.

In addition to an interrogation of the relationship between diaspora and nation, a critical consideration of Filipino youth involvement in DJing also points toward the possibility of redefining the Philippines as the locus not of an orginary and authentic Filipinoness but of a complex history of anticolonial, anticapital struggles and complicities. Soup-a-Crunk discusses Babu's comments in the film *Scratch*, in which he mentions that Filipino youth basically have two role models: their parents and Q-Bert:

SOUP-A-CRUNK: I have not seen the film, so it's kind of out of context. But just by the quote alone, I think it's funny, 'cause in a way, it's kind of true for the younger generation of Filipinos, 'cause that's what's being hyped right now. I think it's true in a sense. It's not just those two who are role models, but definitely they are two strong role models in Filipinos' lives. It's cool to have Q-Bert as a Filipino representative, but then he's not speaking on anything about Filipinos. He's just a Filipino who happened to be a DJ, you know. But it will be another thing if he was, like, wearing this [pointing to a T-shirt he's wearing with the map of the Philippines inscribed on it] while he's doing a competition, like he would speak on something about the Philippines or the conditions or the issues there, right? But I mean, that's not his gig; he's a DJ. Whatever.[7]

While the risk of romanticizing and reifying the Philippines as well as reproducing First World/Third World asymmetries exists, Soup-a-Crunk's view of the Philippines as a site of political identification is suggestive of alternative readings of the "homeland."

In sum, the narratives of my respondents pose a challenge to the notion of a unified Filipino diaspora and monolithic constructions of Filipinoness predicated, in large part, on the experiences of the immigrant generation. Instead, they engage in a kind of cultural politics not easily accommodated in standard diasporic accounts, a kind of cultural politics that dislocates the Philippines as the privileged site of Filipinoness and disengages questions of cultural belonging from conventional markers of Filipinoness. In so doing, my respondents render these markers contingent and negotiable and bring to light alternative forms of identification that are also constitutive of Filipinoness, forms that better accommodate their realities and subjectivities.

But Filipino involvement in DJing can also be problematic in the way it reproduces narrow notions of Filipinoness, particularly along the lines of gender. More to the point, DJ culture constitutes a masculinist space that reflects dominant ideas about gender, although the possibility of reconstituting gendered meanings and identities does exist. Nonetheless, when it comes to gender, it is a mainly conservative arena. In looking to DJing as a vehicle for the assertion of a specifically Filipino identity, Filipino DJs almost always resort to conventional articulations of masculinity. The participation of Filipino youth in this expressive form, therefore, can be read as simultaneously reinforcing and rupturing the normative boundaries of Filipinoness, and as simultaneously recuperating and defamiliarizing conventional markers of Filipinoness. In this sense, diaspora constitutes a contradictory space that disrupts some normative categories while it concomitantly reproduces others.

DJing as an Important Site for Constructing a Distinct Form of Filipino Masculinity

The DJs I interviewed benefit from the aura that has come to surround DJs; they became DJs at a time when DJs enjoy considerable status, substantial influence, and unprecedented popularity. The reputation of DJs, at one point viewed with some suspicion, seems no longer in question. This is the case not just for hip-hop DJs but also for DJs in other genres, like house music.[8] Thus, DJs can now legitimately claim to be artists and musicians, garnering respect and recognition historically reserved for "traditional" musicians. They have become the main draw once again, developing and cultivating their own following. In the case of my respondents, this means that they are no longer seen as merely playing other people's music. Instead, they have become bona fide artists in the eyes of many of their peers.

For my male respondents, DJing serves as a potent source of status and prestige, providing an opportunity to socialize with peers, to meet young women, and to forge networks with other DJs. Echoing the remarks of Rey-Jun and Rygar above, Soup-a-Crunk describes the power and influence that comes with being a DJ:

> INTERVIEWER: People treat you differently because you're a DJ?
> SOUP-A-CRUNK: Yes, they think you're a rock star. No, I mean, really, it's not that extreme. You know, like, most people know you're a DJ, they're super nice to you because they want you to deejay their party for cheap. You know, I'm like, "Hey, I heard this game before. Slow down. Put your brakes on." In that aspect, yes, but then, you know, it's not like I advertised myself as "Oh yeah, by the way, I'm a DJ." It just happens. It's just, like, I mean, I have mixtapes or whatever, but yeah. I mean, girls seem to like it too.
> INTERVIEWER: Talk about that.
> SOUP-A-CRUNK: It's just, like, the idea. They think you know where the parties are, they think you know hella people, they think you know this DJ that DJ and they fucking want you to make mixtapes.[9]

As Soup-a-Crunk alludes to, Filipino DJs' acquisition of subcultural capital is not just based on the kind of services they provide and the kind of skills they possess, but also on what these services and skills signify—connections to the right people, access to parties, and knowledge of the latest trends in music. In effect, involvement in DJing serves as a vehicle for Filipino youth to attain local celebrity status among peers.

The subcultural capital embodied by Filipino DJs also stems, in large part, on their ability to develop a distinctive style that revolves around a particular form of masculinity. In the face of limited means of expression, DJing constitutes one of the few arenas in which Pinoy youth find room to articulate a masculine ideal and publicly display styles of masculinity not generally associated with Filipino men. More specifically, Filipino DJs enact and embody a certain kind of masculinity built around the mastery of technical and musical skills. In their hands, turntables are transformed into musical instruments and, in particular, into sources of innovation and creativity that then serve as the basis of their gender identity. DJing, in other words, has become an important source of status and prestige among Filipino youth precisely because it serves as a vehicle for the production and performance of an emergent Filipino masculinity that resonates with many of them.

In many respects, Filipino DJs subscribe to gender conventions of male performances deployed in other genres of music like rock. In other ways, however, they veer away from these conventions. Compared to rock guitarists, who typically deploy the electric guitar as a phallic symbol, for example, DJs engage in much less blatant hypermasculinist posturing.[10] Nonetheless, for Filipino youth, the manipulation of turntables has come to signify male power and potency through the public display of brown bodies and the expert manipulation of sound technology. To use Steve Waksman's words in another context, the turntable constitutes "both the instrument and the symbol for a highly gendered and racialized form of virtuosity in which the individual player asserted his masculinity as he demonstrated his talent."[11]

But in looking to DJing to construct their own sense of masculine identity, Filipino youth also engage in a set of practices that serves to distinguish themselves from other groups of men. This is evident in the style developed and popularized by Q-Bert, Mix Master Mike, and Apollo, a style that has come to be associated with Filipino DJs and a salient aspect of Filipino DJ performance:

> In 1991, a S.F. crew dubbed FM 2.0 burst onto the national competition circuit. Instead of the flashy acrobatics that were the stock in trade of high-profile competition jocks at the time, members Apollo, Q-Bert, and Mixmaster Mike dazzled judges and audiences with orchestrated scratch routines and tricks developed in the relative isolation of the Bay Area. They took the scene by storm, and after snagging the world championship crown three years in a row, they were asked by the DMC to please bow out of future competitions. Over the course of time, and with the addition of new members, FM 2.0 became the West Coast Rocksteady DJ Crew and eventually Invisbl Skratch Piklz.[12]

For these Pinoy DJs, the emphasis is on the musical aspect of DJing rather than on the performative aspect, on how they sound on stage rather than on how they look as a way to accentuate their creativity and virtuosity. In their view, too much focus on what Reighley describes as "flashy acrobatics," a style of DJing that tends to be associated with black DJs, detracts from the musicianship of DJs.

In emphasizing this aspect of DJing, Filipino DJs are cultivating their own sense of masculine identity that is not simply an attempt to replicate black masculine style or appropriate signifiers of black masculinity. Instead, they distinguish their style from black performance style as a way to define themselves as musicians first and performers second, which then serves as the basis of an emergent Filipino masculinity. Through their creative engagement with sound technology, then, Filipino DJs are reconfiguring particular codes and conventions of performance style into signifiers of Filipino masculinity and opening up space for Filipino youth to imagine and affirm an alternative conception of Filipino manhood.

Filipino youth also look to DJing as a means of articulating a distinct sense of gender identity that is not consistent or congruent with the masculinity embodied by first-generation Filipino men. As a number of feminist scholars of color have noted, migration brings about shifts in gender, generational relations, and power, including changes in the status of male and female migrants and their children. Migration restructures family relations, creating opportunities to renegotiate gender roles and expectations, including meanings of masculinity and femininity, while simultaneously reinforcing patriarchy. On the one hand, women often gain status and power but also shoulder added burdens. Likewise, children gain status and power. On the other hand, men often lose status and power at the same time that they continue to benefit from their status as men, as they no longer have access to social and cultural resources that had previously underwritten their authority.[13]

For first-generation Filipino men, migration often results in downward occupational mobility that, in turn, undermines the basis of their masculinity. This is the case, for example, for Filipino men in the U.S. Navy, who have been largely confined to the ranks of officers' steward and mess attendant, which many of them perceive as an affront to their dignity and self-worth. According to Espiritu, "the experiences of these Navy men underscore the fact that for many immigrants, the experience of migration is most often a compromise: although their wages may be higher, their status is not, and their dignity suffers."[14] Denied access to decent-paying and high-status jobs and other forms of institutional power, first-generation Filipino men fail to live up to established definitions of masculinity. In response, these men look to other spheres to recoup their masculinity, an effort that more often than not reinforces patriarchy.[15]

Within this context, then, Filipino youth participation in DJing can be seen as providing an alternative and appealing path to the kind of professional or service work awaiting Filipino men. It offers them an alternative source of status that allows them to enact a kind of masculinity distinct from the masculinity embodied by first-generation Filipino men, a kind of masculinity not strictly associated with or contingent on the kind of work first-generation Filipino men are engaged in. DJing, in other words, makes possible the rejection of regulated forms of labor and enables Pinoy youth to experience their bodies not just as instruments of labor but also as sources of pleasure and sensuality and, in the process, counteract the low cultural capital historically associated with Filipino bodies.[16]

Q-Bert's popularity is particularly instructive in terms of illuminating issues of gender identification and masculinity among Filipino youth who hardly have any successful role models whose experiences resonate with their own. In the eyes of Filipino youth, Q-Bert has become a source of racial and masculine pride, a groundbreaking DJ who elevated the art and practice of DJing and paved the way for the next generation of Filipino DJs. As several of my respondents point out, it is largely through his accomplishments that Filipinos have gained a reputation for being the best DJs in the world. They look to Q-Bert as embodying new ways of being Filipino in the United States and foregrounding the potential of DJing as a vehicle for achieving notoriety and credibility. In so doing, he has helped transform DJing into one of the few spaces in which Filipino youth could wield a certain amount of power and authority and represent themselves on their own terms.

At another level, Q-Bert's popularity is grounded in his ability to embody an idealized form of masculinity that resonates with Filipino youth in the United States. This is significant in light of the dearth of appealing images of Filipino men. Filipino youth identification with Q-Bert, however, is not just based on his exceptional skills but also on his ability to evoke the "ordinary":

> RYGAR: Well, like someone said at a PAA meeting, Q-Bert is up there; he's the man when it comes to scratching. So, and he represents the Filipino community you know—he's like a typical, short Filipino DJ. But the thing is, he's doing these commercials, and people that know him are going to be like, "Damn, there's Q-Bert. He came up." He's just representing the Filipinos in the community that, 'cause him being the best, just basically says that Filipinos, like, uh, they're pretty much in the hip-hop scene, you know.[17]

Filipino youth identify with Q-Bert because in many respects, he is "one of them" in terms of physical stature as Rygar points out but also in terms of personal history. Like many of them, for example, Q-Bert grew up in the Bay Area and, until recently, continued to live in the region even after his initial success. It is this sense of "ordinariness" that, in many ways, serves to underscore his authenticity and validate him as a genuine embodiment of Filipinoness. Part of Q-Bert's allure, therefore, is not just a function of extraordinary skills but also of his "non-exceptional" nature.

Pinay Youth Exclusion and Marginalization within DJ Culture

Like Pinoy DJs, the Pinay DJs I interviewed are drawn to the music, power, and energy of DJ culture. Notwithstanding the similarities, however, their personal narratives reveal profound differences in terms of their experiences within DJ culture, differences rooted in the masculinist orientation of DJ culture but also mainstream gender norms that further serve to delimit Pinay youth participation in DJing. For one thing, men have more mobility and access to public urban spaces than do women, and therefore men have more opportunities to engage publicly in youth culture and to make money. Conversely, women are required to do unpaid labor within the home that is simply not expected of young men. Thus, female youth participation in DJing has been largely confined to that of consumers rather than active producers of the culture.

While the Pinoy DJs I interviewed are quick to acknowledge the dearth of female DJs, they generally do not consider the issue particularly relevant or important. This is in contrast to the Pinay DJs I interviewed, who are fully aware of the way gender structures the participation of female DJs in different ways from those of male DJs, as reflected in their marginal status within the culture. They are especially conscious and made conscious of those practices and discourses that render their legitimacy contingent and provisional. Nonetheless, like their male counterparts, they look to DJing as a site generating new possibilities for gender identification. In other words, the masculinist orientation of DJing does not preclude the construction of alternative femininities.

Aspiring DJs learn the basics of DJing through collective practices—for example, a group of friends will pool their resources, including equipment, money, and records; or an aspiring DJ will rely on more established DJs for guidance and mentorship. For the most part, however, these avenues or modes of skill acquisition have been foreclosed to my female respondents:

> INTERVIEWER: In terms of learning how to DJ, were you taught by other DJs, or was it mostly you and your friends picking things up and learning on your own?
>
> CELSKIII: There were not too many people who helped us besides Piklz, 'cause you know, a lot of the guys are assholes and would say . . .
>
> INTERVIEWER: Let's talk about that.
>
> CELSKIII: They were assholes. They were not helpful, even my friends who are DJs and they are guys. I learned pretty much on my own. I think that's the only way, to find your own sound. You fuck with it however long it takes to finally come up with your own style.
>
> INTERVIEWER: So you asked your DJ friends if they could . . .
>
> CELSKIII: When I was getting turntables I did not know what to buy. I did not even know there was a difference between direct drive and belt drive. I did not even know that different would get you different things. So I was asking my friend who was a DJ, "Oh, what do I need to buy?" And he was shady from the

beginning. He was like, "It does not matter. You could get that." With the set I ended up getting, it was the worst set you could ever get. Well he was like, "This is good for mixing." It seemed like he was purposely even trying to limit me from what I could do. And then when I got my turntables too, I was like, "Oh, I don't know what to do. How do I set it up?" He came over and he was not really helpful. He set it up and he really did not explain it, and so I had to figure it out myself.

INTERVIEWER: You think if you were guy that would have made a difference? You think these people you asked would have been more helpful?

CELSKIII: Yeah, definitely. I guess with him and some of my other friends, they did not think I'm serious about it. If it was a guy, they'll be more willing to help. With anything though, when it comes to handling technology, there's doubt that women can actually work it, the equipment.[18]

Generally excluded from social networks that have paved the way for the next generation of Filipino DJs, the Pinay DJs I interviewed have had to essentially learn the basics of DJing on their own, which serves to ensure that the preponderance of DJs and DJ crews are men.

It is not surprising, therefore, to hear female respondents talk about the dearth of female DJs they could look up to and emulate. One Tyme discusses the influence of one of the few female DJs in the culture but also laments the absence of female DJs:

INTERVIEWER: Did Pinay DJs influence you at all, Pinay DJs like Symphony?

ONE TYME: Kuttin' Kandi. When I first saw her at a DMC, I was like, "I want to be exactly like her." And after that, I've never heard about her anymore. It's kind of depressing because all I see are males up there on turntables. There's DJ Shortee, and like Symphony, I don't think she's in it anymore. Kuttin' Kandi, I haven't heard anything about her.

INTERVIEWER: So Kuttin' Kandi really made an impression on you?

ONE TYME: Yeah, like, once I saw there's a female on turntables, I wanted to be exactly like her. I wanted to be in DMCs, beat juggling and all that. But of course everything changed and I got more into mixing and production. I still want to learn that aspect focusing on production.[19]

The absence of female DJs means that Pinay youth are primarily exposed to male DJs, which can serve to discourage them and other female youth from pursuing DJing. In One Tyme's case, seeing a Pinay DJ perform on stage clearly made a difference in her decision to take up DJing, though it was also difficult for her to come up with more than a handful of names of prominent female DJs.

A common theme that emerges in the personal narratives of Pinay DJs is that they are taken much less seriously than their male counterparts, and they have to deal with a lack of respect for their musical abilities. The female respondents recalled a number of instances in which they had to perform under intense scrutiny from male peers:

> CELSKIII: There's a lot of sexism in hip-hop, period. There's a lot in every element, in DJing too. That's one of the biggest issues that you deal with. We always get comments from guys, comments about . . . you know, people think either we're, they're doubtful of our skills until we get on and do what we do, but before that, they have all these questions, like, trying to test. So we're always getting tested, basically, even when we go record shopping.[20]
>
> ONE TYME: From other DJs? They're just really critical. They, every single move you make, every single beat, "Oh, that's off beat. That does not blend well. What is she doing? She can't scratch." They're really critical. When they see a female DJ up there, they're really critical. If they don't know you're a female, like you're upstairs, they'll just . . . once they find out, they listen really carefully to your mixing.[21]

Perceived as intruding in a masculine space, Pinay DJs are not accorded authenticity in the same way as their male peers. Instead, they are evaluated more intensely, perceived as not taking the art and craft of DJing seriously, and incapable of delivering a technically skilled performance. Within DJing, therefore, authenticity is not something everyone can claim. Instead, it is defined in masculine terms and remains the prerogative of men.[22]

The kind of authenticity at play within DJ culture is grounded in the notion that female DJs are unable and unwilling to put in the time and effort necessary to excel in DJing. Consequently, Pinay DJs are not evaluated according to the same criteria as male DJs. Instead, they must demonstrate their competence in ways not required of men. This is evident in audience expectations of female DJs as described by Rey-Jun and One Tyme:

> INTERVIEWER: Have you been to competitions with female DJs competing?
> REY-JUN: Yeah, I saw Pam the Funkstress competing at the DMC.
> INTERVIEWER: Was the audience responding differently to her because she was female?
> REY-JUN: Yeah, definitely. Not even Pam the Funkstress, but Symphony, who's with the Beat Junkies. She was in this thing in LA.
> INTERVIEWER: So, talk about the audience response to them.
> REY-JUN: It was more of a shock factor, but it was also support. I think that's why they get so much reaction. They get a lot of reaction and lot of support in their routines, because they scratch with their breasts.
> INTERVIEWER: So when it comes to audience reaction, skills don't matter as much.

REY-JUN: Yeah, just as long as they're trying.

INTERVIEWER: So if it was a guy, he would have been booed.

REY-JUN: Oh yeah, but Symphony got skills. I thought she was good.[23]

INTERVIEWER: When you're hired, what are the expectations?

ONE TYME: I don't know, I don't know what they expect when they hire us. I have no clue what they expect of us, probably like tits and ass, I guess, like, that's what they expect to see.[24]

Unlike male DJs, female DJs are evaluated primarily on the basis of their looks and, more specifically, what they are willing to show. DJ skills, as both One Tyme and Rey-Jun point out, do not seem to matter when it comes to female DJs, who are considered legitimate only if they show skin.[25]

Also stemming from the perceived lack of authenticity of female DJs is the notion that female participation in DJ culture is contingent on their affiliation with males and, in particular, intimate relationships with men. According to this line of thinking, Pinay DJs are nothing but ancillary members of the culture, drawn to DJing only because their boyfriends are involved, and therefore, their commitment to the culture is viewed as superficial and ephemeral:

REY-JUN: I think a lot of reasons some girls are into it is because their friends are into it, or their boyfriends are into it. Like Shortee, her boyfriend was into it big time. That's how they hooked up.[26]

TEASE: I've a hard time getting into a club. I'd be wheeling in my records, and security will be like, "Where's your boyfriend?" and I'm like, "Excuse me?" "Are you the DJ's girlfriend?" "No, I'm the DJ." "Oh, hold on. Let me call the promoter." So I'm here, and he's looking back at the . . . I'm on the cell phone going, "Fucker, get me in. Your security is giving me a fucking hard ass time."[27]

Overlooked, then, are the ways Pinay DJs exercise agency—their own reasons for becoming DJs, how they negotiate with DJ culture's masculinist prerogative in contradictory and complex ways, and the significance of DJing in affording young women a space to call into being alternative forms of womanhood and sexuality.[28]

Another theme that emerges in the personal narratives of Pinay DJs is lack of parental support and encouragement. For the parents of my female respondents, DJing constitutes a male activity, and thus, they pressure their daughters to pursue what they as gender appropriate behavior:

ONE TYME: Support of family, I think, is a big thing. 'Cause, like, a lot of my friends tell me, "Oh, your parents support you. Really?" They're so surprised about it. They're like, "My parents would never buy me turntables. My parents, they think it's a waste of money and all that." And like, just basically support, 'cause I think that's why I've gotten so far, because a lot of people support me on it, especially my parents. They know it's a male-dominated thing. I guess it all falls on their family. "Why do you want to do this? Are you a tomboy 'cause you're doing this or something." Like, I've gotten that from my family before, like, my relatives. It's like, this is what I love to do. It's like, my parents support me on it, and that's all I really care about, like, what I want to do.[29]

CELSKIII: There's not a lot of female musicians in the world, period. In any music genre, especially in hip-hop, there's lack of representation. Maybe because it's that kind of discouragement, and women are not encouraged to be creative, Filipinos like my dad saying, oh, I need to study. I need to do this and that. There's already this expected lifestyle that we're expected to have, and there's no room for any kind of creative expression usually. So I think that already sets a problem up, like, a lot of women probably don't even think that they can, that they have the time for that, that they cannot do it period. With Filipinas, there's a handful of us. It's already an unsaid . . . an arena for guys.[30]

As evident in the above narratives, Filipina youth involvement in DJ culture is shaped not only by gender conventions and heterosexual norms within DJ culture but also by parenting practices within the family underwritten by normative notions of Filipinaness. Accordingly, pursuing DJing is viewed as a transgression of the normative boundaries of Filipinaness, casting their femininity in doubt.

This is in stark contrast to the parental support and encouragement Pinoy DJs generally receive, in the form of permission to stay out all night, money to buy DJ equipment, and encouragement to practice and hone their DJ skills. Statistix's father, for example, bought him sound equipment—an amplifier, speakers, and a turntable—costing about $3,000 after realizing how much DJing meant to him. Likewise, Rey-Jun's parents bought him his first turntables for earning good grades and graduating junior high. Celskiii, however, had to come up with the money herself:

INTERVIEWER: Going back to how you came up with the money to buy your first set of turntables, it came mainly from working at McDonald's?

CELSKIII: I had to save it because my parents would not buy it for me. My mom thought I was crazy, and my dad said it was for guys. And so I just saved up for myself.[31]

As evidenced by the foregoing, Pinoy youth involvement in DJing is almost always met with parental approval, because of the way it is seen as compatible with normative notions of Filipinoness. On the contrary, the parents of Pinay DJs generally viewed their involvement in DJing with disapproval and suspicion, because is it seen as incompatible with normative notions of Filipinaness.

Not surprisingly, the, Pinay youth involvement in DJing was often a source of friction between them and their parents. Celskiii recounts her frayed relationship with her father:

> CELSKIII: My dad, he always had a problem with it. He thought it was a waste of time and money. And he also thinks that it's for boys. He always said that to me. My mom, she's a little more supportive. They got used to it because I played music loud anyways before I had the turntables. So it was something my mom tries to get used to, but she's supportive of me. My friends would come over, and we'll practice, and she was cool with it. My dad was like, "You need to study. That's not for you. Why don't you play the piano?" He said that because before the turntables I took piano lessons, but I did not like it. And then my sister played the piano. I would always say, "Oh, it's an instrument, Dad." And then my dad would always say, "Oh no, the piano, play the piano."[32]

In Tease's case, her father was generally supportive of her involvement in DJing but not her mother:

> TEASE: My mom, on the other hand, she hated the idea. She was like, "No, it's a male-dominated thing. DJing is for men. I'm like, "Mom, you're tripping." So I guess another reason why I continue to deejay is because I wanted to piss her off.[33]

Perceived by my respondents' parents as a "male thing," DJing becomes a highly contested arena in which to express, debate, and challenge ideas concerning the boundaries of Filipina womanhood.

In many ways, parental objections to the involvement of their daughters in DJing resonate with ideologies of female domesticity that delimit female musicianship within the confines of the family and discourage the pursuit of music as a career. Music, in other words, should only be pursued as long as it fulfills a service function within the home—for example, entertaining family or guests. Related to this is the coding of particular musical instruments as suitable vehicles for the expression of female subjectivity and creativity. Celskiii's father, for example, encouraged her to play the piano, a musical instrument historically coded as appropriate for women because of its compatibility with the ideal of female domesticity. At the same time, he discouraged her from playing turntables because he considered it an inappropriate form of female musical expression.[34]

Parental objections to daughters becoming DJs also resonate with the narrative of female morality valorized in many Filipino families, a narrative underwritten by an idealized image of Filipinaness. DJing is considered an inappropriate activity for Pinay youth to pursue because it means engaging in practices—going out and staying out late, frequenting places deemed "unsafe" and "dangerous" for women, and being around male peers—that purportedly pose a threat to Pinay virtue. Pinay youth involvement in DJing, then, makes it difficult for parent to control and regulate their daughters' behavior as well as to keep tabs on their daughters' whereabouts and confine them to the domestic sphere.

Moreover, Pinay youth pursuit of DJing as a career disrupts the model minority expectations of their parents, who expect their daughters to get good grades in school and pursue what they consider more legitimate career paths. Celskiii's parents, for example, wanted her to become a lawyer or a teacher, but as evidenced in the following, Celskiii does not subscribe to the notion that education is the key to social mobility because of the way it forecloses other possibilities:

> INTERVIEWER: What does he [father] want you to do instead?
>
> CELSKIII: A lawyer, a teacher. I just told them, "Yeah, don't worry. You got *ate* [older sister] to support you." With parents, I don't know. My mom is supportive. She knows that it can happen, 'cause she talks to Q's [Q-Bert's] mom. His situation was even worse. He was an "F" student. They were not supportive. They were on his back 'cause he's the only child. Now they are all like happy for him, showing him off. But my mom knows it's what makes me happy. I think that's why she's chill about it.
>
> INTERVIEWER: Maybe your dad needs to talk to Q's mom.
>
> CELSKIII: My dad does not get involved, period. Mix Master Mike used to live down the street from my house in Vallejo, and I used to go, "Yeah, you know Mix Master Mike? Look at him, Dad. You see, he's Filipino. You see what he's doing." And he said, "Didn't I see him in Vallejo?" I said, "You don't need to have this lifestyle." The working class, they really believe that you could mobilize straight up with education, that you could move from the working class.[35]

For Celskiii, it is not about making money or becoming rich but making enough money to survive while doing something she loves. From this perspective, then, DJing provides an appealing alternative to the model minority expectations of her parents.

DJing as a Site for Negotiating Gender Conventions and Sexual Norms

Female DJs' views of themselves are not concurrent with male DJs' or parents' views of them. This is evident in the different ways Pinay DJs have responded to and challenged the masculinist presumptions of DJing in subtle and ambivalent ways. Engaging in their own gendered performances, they have contested preconceived notions of female musicianship and problematized the different criteria by which male DJs and female DJs are evaluated, while at the same time challenging idealized notions of Filipinaness. In others words, DJing offers a venue to counteract normative models of Filipino womanhood rooted in DJ culture and the deployment of culture and tradition in the diaspora.

Perceived as intruding in a male realm, female DJs constantly deal with disparaging remarks and furtive looks that cast their legitimacy and credibility as DJs in doubt. My female respondents recounted a number of these incidents, for which they developed and used effective one-line retorts. Celskiii came up with a way to counteract verbal forms of harassment from make DJs, forms of harassment that have become routine in DJ culture:

> CELSKIII: There were so many things. "You're good for a girl, but you need to learn how to control that fader more," or things like that, belittling us because they were threatened. That was before. Like, now when I get those comments I learn how to quick-wit and shoot back at them. Like, this year we were mixing and something was wrong with my needle, and one of the guys was like, "Oh, why don't you take it out and lick it." And the way he even said that I was pissed. I just looked at him and said, "Why don't you show me how to do that. I know you know how to do that." It's just like learning. A lot of times some of the shows are really sexist, and we have to perform at these shows. I just keep in mind a lot of them are ignorant. And I don't want it to affect how I play. So I'm just mindful.[36]

Accustomed to receiving verbal insults, Celskiii has learned to not let these kinds of comments affect her performance. Instead, she has made a calculated and self-conscious decision to respond to disparaging remarks, making sure that male DJs do not have the last word.

In counteracting verbal forms of harassment, Celskiii is not only staking out her place within DJing but also negotiating what it means to be Filipina. DJing serves as a means of going against parental expectations and demands of domesticity and upward mobility and asserting an alternative model of Filipina womanhood:

> CELSKIII: What I learned from Q and them is that you can live like that, you can live a slave to the role you're supposed to, that everyone expects you to have, or you can make a living from something that makes you happy. That's something my parents never really gave me, that choice. It was just school. It was already expected—get married, have a family. But that's not what I want to do. I don't want to go to school and then have a family. There's so much that you could do, and I think music is one of the ways that can take you to experience other things in life. So I think DJing, it's been something that kept me learning outside of school until I started to learn more—from the music I picked up,

from the people around DJing—you learn about music, you learn about the history, you learn about what is it about scratching like . . . rhythm, syncopation. Even in your philosophy of playing music, you start to apply it to everything else you have in your life. Like the energy I put into my music, I could put this energy to other things too. It shaped who I am today and through doing music and on my own, too, because my parents were not there.[37]

Refusing to be confined to the domestic sphere or to be defined by history and tradition, Celskiii unsettles the normative boundaries of Filipino womanhood and challenges the gender proscriptions of Filipino culture. Taking up DJing becomes a way to envision a different kind of life for herself, one that does not revolve primarily around school, marriage, and having a family. In this light, DJing provides an appealing alternative, offering the possibility of fulfillment and living her life on her own terms.

Like Celskiii, Deeandroid finds that her participation in DJing enables her to unsettle gender-based expectations, what constitutes "proper" and "acceptable" behavior on the part of female youth. In the following, she questions conventional norms of femininity that call for a preoccupation with physical appearance and self-image:

DEEANDROID: Like, uh, there's always been some kind of uncomfortable feelings between Pinays, you know, if you don't know them. A lot of Pinays are snobby to each other. I guess it has to do with personal issues too. Growing up, you know, being comfortable with yourself and how you look. You know, a lot of Pinays focus on how they look, and that's what makes them feel good about themselves. I don't focus so much on that, but when I see Pinays I know that there's those uncomfortable things, so I know what not to do to make beef.[38]

In rejecting a conventional marker of femininity, Deeandroid manages to reformulate conventional notions of feminine appeal and appearance. In so doing, she not only expresses herself in nonstereotypical feminine ways, but also brings attention to the production and performance of competing articulations of Filipinaness.

In the case of One Tyme, she uses clothing to negotiate the masculinist orientation of DJ culture and cultivate an appearance that frustrates expectations of female performance. Her reliance on commodities to carve out a niche evokes a fairly standard practice in hip-hop, as participants strive to claim a higher status through the conspicuous consumption of clothing and other accessories. It speaks to the power of consumption as a means of cultural contestation. In this instance, One Tyme's use of clothing plays not only on class distinctions and hierarchies but also gender distinctions and hierarchies.[39]

For One Tyme, becoming a DJ does not mean that she has to cater to crowd expectations and show skin, as reflected in her choice of fashion and style to negotiate her gender identity and carve out her own niche within DJing:

> ONE TYME: We've been to a few car shows, like, we deejayed at car shows just, like, for promotion. A lot of girls in our group dress provocatively; they think they're models or whatever. It's like, "Oh wow." My manager even told me, 'cause usually I dress how I dress, like I dress jeans and a shirt, and she's like, "The only reason why a lot of guys came to our table cause like they saw ladies showing their breasts," not showing but, you know . . . [40]

Here, One Tyme wears clothes she is comfortable in—jeans and a shirt—which are standard gear for male DJs but not for female DJs, who are expected to wear revealing clothing. In effect, she uses markers of masculinity and male identity as part of her self-presentation to accentuate her technical skills rather than physical attractiveness and to project a different kind of image that does not live up to gendered expectations.

The prevailing gender discourse in DJ culture dictates that female creativity and subjectivity can only be legitimately expressed if female DJs show skin. It is not surprising, therefore, to see provocatively dressed female DJs attract crowds. Nonetheless, One Tyme manages to attract crowds on the basis of her skills:

> ONE TYME: Yeah, they're like, "The only reason why they came to see us spin and all that . . . like, you have the biggest crowd there and it's like they were listening to your skills and all that and what you were playing instead of just looking at you." [41]

By adopting "male" gear, One Tyme is defying expectations of female performance and challenging norms of female display predicated on showing skin. In her self-representation, she broadens the range of femininities articulated within DJing, recasting what it means to be a female DJ and a Pinay DJ in a male-dominated realm. By the same token, One Tyme demonstrates that physical appearance is not the only source of cultural authority and power in DJing for Pinay youth.

In contrast to One Tyme, Tease has made a calculated and self-conscious decision to wear provocative clothing that accentuates the contours of her body. For her, presenting herself this way has become a vehicle for self-promotion:

> TEASE: Drunk club heads, especially when I'd deejay and stuff, I'd be total eye candy. I'd show cleavage just to tease the crowd. I don't give a fuck.

INTERVIEWER: So that's intentional on your part?

TEASE: That's intentional on my part, to be like, "Hey, I'm a woman hear me roar." And if they look at it, they look at it. They see it, they would be like, "Cool," just make them think it is cool.[42]

Tease is well aware of audience expectations when it comes to female DJs, exploiting the masculinist orientation of DJing to her own advantage. Her choice of clothing, however, can be read as subscribing to conventional views of femininity in the way she performs a compulsory feminine identity and acquiesces to demands of physical display.

But as evident in the following, Tease also wants to be recognized not just for her looks but also for her DJ skills. Like female musicians in other genres of music, Tease is grappling with the complexities and contradictions of female self-representation in a male-dominated realm, wanting to avoid being seen as merely eye candy but also wanting "to be known as a DJ who is good and not because I'm just a girl":

INTERVIEWER: And if people hire you strictly based on looks, that's fine with you?

TEASE: Hold on, let me think about that. I would be concerned, but at the same time, I know that I have the skills. I want to be known as a good DJ, not because I'm a girl. I mean, if I get hired because of looks over my skills, that has happened a couple of time. In a DJ lineup, they'll get really good DJs and stuff, but then I'll be hired over this guy DJ because I was a girl. But it's part of the game. The promoter wants to attract people, and putting a girl in the lineup is one of them, you know. It's a business thing. It's not personal; it's a business. That's one of my lines: it's not personal; it's a business.

INTERVIEWER: Isn't showing cleavage going against your goal to be recognized for your DJ skills?

TEASE: I think I'm using it to my advantage. I mean I want to be recognized as a DJ and I'm female. Sorry, I should've said instead of a female DJ. As I said, I want to be good, I want to be known as a DJ who is good and not because I'm just a girl. And I'm using it to my advantage, me, maybe being attractive to come up in the DJ scene and stuff like that. I mean my mix show coordinator told me it's like, "Hey, people want to hire you because they heard of a girl DJ, but they barely saw you, and when they saw you, they're like hell yeah, put her in the lineup."[43]

On the one hand, Tease realizes that wearing revealing clothing is an effective vehicle for self-promotion. On the other hand, she realizes that presenting herself provocatively and engaging in a performance of sexuality that subscribes to established conventions may work against her wish to be recognized as a bona fide DJ.[44]

In addition to individual acts, Pinay DJs also engage in collective acts in order to carve out a space for female creativity and subjectivity. A couple of the Pinay DJs I interviewed, for example, are part of an all female multiracial DJ crew called Divas of Style Entertainment (DOSE). One Tyme talks about the focus and purpose of the group:

> ONE TYME: It's called Divas of Style Entertainment. It does not really focus on hip-hop. It's focused on mainstream and all that. I'm labeled their underground hip-hop DJ, turntablist. I wanted to join the group because it's for females and like, I've never seen anything like that before. Like, the model I guess you can say we go by is like, we don't want to be seen: "Oh, she's good for a girl." We want to be seen: "She's good." And then, like, they look up and, "Oh, she's a girl." That's what I really dig about it. It's like, we want to be known for our techniques before even being seen as a girl because, like, it's a male-dominated scene.[45]

As one of the few all-female DJ crews, DOSE functions as both a performing unit and a creative unit. It provides a supportive environment in which female DJs could be taken seriously and encouraged to develop and hone their skills, disrupting the notion that female participation is contingent on male affiliation. Moreover, the collective serves as a forum in which group members affirm the legitimacy and credibility of female DJs as musicians and active participants in the culture.

DOSE strives to eventually achieve the same level of prominence as SBC and Spintronix, crews that One Tyme describes as the "big boys." However, in the highly competitive field of DJing, DOSE has to compete with not only more established DJ crews, but also up-and-coming DJ crews comprising primarily male DJs who, by virtue of their gender identity, are at advantage when it comes to securing gigs. Thus, it has not been that easy for the group to get gigs. Moreover, One Tyme points out that the group generally receives lower pay than their male counterparts for providing the same kind of service:

> INTERVIEWER: As one of the few Pinay DJs out there, what kinds of obstacles have you had to deal with that you would not if you were male?
> ONE TYME: Pay is one thing. Males can get two hundred dollars more easily over a female.
> INTERVIEWER: Really?
> ONE TYME: Yeah, and, like, you could be as good as males and all that, but they still get a lot more than female DJs do. Our crew, like Divas of Style, they get less that compared to SBC crew. Like, they have been around, but I think we both have the same talent. And they're still getting, like, thousand-dollar gigs and we're over here busting our ass for eight-hundred-dollar gigs and all that.

And like, and just how people look at you. It's like, "Oh, she's a girl. She can't do it as good as the guy 'cause she's just a girl." And like we're trying to break that stereotype and all that.[46]

The perceived lack of authenticity of female DJs means that DOSE DJs not only have to deal with skepticism regarding their DJ skills but also lack of financial remuneration relative to their male counterparts.

Yet DOSE members are also well aware of the novelty of women DJs, and thus they make a concerted effort to capitalize on the masculinist orientation of DJing by redeploying and rearticulating their sexuality in strategic ways. As One Tyme notes, several DOSE DJs don revealing clothing as a way to bring attention to the group, secure gigs, and attract a large following or audience. In this respect, then, the decision of some group members to dress provocatively may very well help the group achieve prominence in the field of DJing. By the same token, it may very well compromise the other objective of the group—to be seen as bona fide DJs or musicians.

Very much conscious of and concerned with the dearth of female DJs, the Pinay DJs I interviewed have made a concerted effort to encourage and mentor aspiring female DJs:

> INTERVIEWER: Is there a conscious effort on your part to mentor Filipinas?
> CELSKIII: . . . So like when I meet people when we're doing shows, some women would go up to us, "Oh, you know that was dope." It's cool, because they can appreciate the music. I also see how it makes a difference when they see a woman up there. Some of them do get inspired. So it's always, like, we'll give them our e-mail address, and I always tell them, "Yeah, if you guys want to learn, we can help you." And then we also did a workshop for, like, young women of color. It was, like, a lot of girls from the projects, not necessarily Filipino. A lot of them were black and Latina. So we did that.[47]

As some of the few female DJs in the culture, several of my female respondents have made it a point to do whatever they can to help female youth get into DJing, as they are fully cognizant of the difference mentorship makes particularly for aspiring female DJs.

Through their efforts to carve out a niche within DJ culture, Pinay DJs have opened up new possibilities for aspiring women DJs, legitimizing the involvement of women in DJing and broadening the range of femininities articulated in DJing. More specifically, Pinay DJs enact and perform an alternative kind of femininity that, to use Norma Mendoza-Denton's words, "not only confounds wider community notions of how girls should act, dress, and talk, but throws into question the very gendered category that girls are expected to inhabit."[48] They demonstrate that it is possible for women to assert themselves through DJing and that DJing is not simply an inherently male form, but rather, its meanings and uses can be appropriated to serve as a source of empowerment for female youth. By the same token, Pinay DJs demonstrate that performance expressions need not be restricted to the domestic sphere, and in the process they open up a space for female youth as active participants in the production of youth culture.

But the personal narratives of Pinay DJs also demonstrate that by engaging in self-definition, they not only unsettle conventional expectations regarding what it means to be a female DJ but also what it means to be Filipina. Just as Pinoy youth look to DJing to construct an alternative form of Filipino masculinity, Pinay youth look to DJing to construct an alternative form of femininity that does not conform to normative models of Filipina womanhood, which are rooted in domesticity and bound up with patriarchal notions of family, sexuality, and gender. More specifically, DJing allows them to defy parental expectations of how a "good" daughter should behave and redraw the boundaries of Pinay propriety and comportment, and in the process, broaden the range of identities that Pinay youth can enact.

Through their involvement in DJing, Pinay DJs are able to counteract parental limitations on their autonomy and mobility that often dictate when and where leisure activities can take place. It allows them to counteract burdens placed on Filipina daughters to carry on cultural traditions. By staying out late, frequenting spaces considered unsafe, and taking part in activities considered inappropriate, they are able to mitigate parental control over their bodies and the strict moral codes underlying this control. And by challenging their confinement to domesticity, Pinay DJs are able to assert their presence in public spaces and stake out public identities that, in turn, destabilize the construction of the "home in feminine terms as a 'safe' haven and the public sphere of the streets as 'dangerous' or 'male' terrain."[49] In so doing, they expand and reconfigure signifiers of Filipinaness so that it is no longer defined exclusively in terms of chastity, sexual modesty, and dedication to the family.

This is not to say that Pinay DJs do not reproduce many aspects of conventional gender norms or participate in their own subordination at the same time that they challenge it. In their struggles to prove that they belong, Pinay DJs, at times, reinforce rather than provide an alternative to prescribed meanings of femininity, affirming the very relations they seek to subvert. The complicity of Pinay DJs, however, says less about the politics they subscribe to and more about the constraints they have to deal with in order to carve out a niche in DJing, and it also says less about the strategies they engage in and more about the difficulty of imagining alternative models of femininity outside the bounds of patriarchy.

Conclusion **Reimagining the Hip-hop Nation**

> We like France for what it is but we can't say the flag "blue, white, red" really represents us. Our flag is hip-hop.
>
> Phase-T dancer, *Planet B-Boy*, 2007

IT HAS NOW BECOME COMMONPLACE to refer to hip-hop and its constituency as part of a nation: the hip-hop nation. In an article on hip-hop nationalism, Jeffrey Louis Decker traces the initial usage of the phrase "hip-hop nation" to a *Village Voice* article published January 19, 1988. Since its initial usage, the term "hip-hop nation" has enjoyed a great deal of currency, and is a phrase often invoked in both popular and scholarly accounts of hip-hop. Halifu Osumare, for example, speaks of the political and economic clout of the hip-hop nation and how it has evolved into a force to be reckoned with on a global scale, while Russel A. Porter and Benito M. Vergara speak of the expanding boundaries of the hip-hop nation, which has come to encompass various groups.[1] Along the same lines, Shuhei Hosokowa speaks of a "translocal hip-hop nation" that has generated a strong sense of allegiance among Japanese MCs in his discussion of the Japanese rap scene, while David Grazian speaks of how the hip-hop nation shares markers of authenticity with the blues.[2]

Uttered by one of the b-boys for the French b-boy crew represented in the film *Planet B-Boy*,[3] the quote that opens this chapter speaks to the global scope and reach of hip-hop, as well as the growing resonance and rhetorical power of the notion of hip-hop nation to youth worldwide. Phase-T speaks to the ways hip-hop has generated a strong sense of identity and allegiance among youth in different parts of the globe, seemingly superseding their allegiance to their nations of origin and residence.

At the same time, the Phase-T's insight speaks to the tenuousness of nationalist narratives predicated on the unity of national subjects and, more

89

specifically, on the ambivalent relationship between b-boy crews like Phase-T, composed primarily of African b-boys, and a nation like France. As another member of the crew points out, "We come from so many backgrounds in France the phrase 'French culture' doesn't really apply."[4] It speaks to the deployment of hip-hop to challenge official nationalist narratives and discourses and think through the politics of belonging within the context of the nation-state.

These sentiments from members of Phase-T, however, also raise a set of questions pertinent to this book: What is it about hip-hop that compels these French b-boys to swear their allegiance to the "flag" of hip-hop? What accounts for the appeal of "nation?" How is the hip-hop nation imagined in different parts of the globe? What are the shared myths and symbols of this nation? Why deploy the frame and trope of nation in relation to an expressive form that is undoubtedly global in scope? How is race implicated in conceptualizations of the hip-hop nation? How is membership understood? Is deracination a prerequisite of membership? In what ways does the notion of hip-hop nation fit with conventional definitions of nation?

In this concluding chapter, I provide a critical interrogation of the deployment of the trope "nation" within hip-hop through a consideration of how nation is implicated in b-boy culture as articulated in the film *Planet B-Boy*. I am particularly interested in how nation is conceptualized and the ways it is complicit with conventional nationalist discourse and logic. Building on the works of a cohort of Filipino American cultural critics, I conclude the chapter with a discussion of how DJing fits in relation to the wide array of cultural forms and practices that compose the terrain of Filipino popular culture. I explore the ways Filipino American cultural productions constitute an engagement with nation that is neither simple nor straightforward.

Planet B-Boy and the Global Hip-hop Nation

Revolving around the 2005 Battle of the Year, a b-boy competition that involves the participation of b-boy crews all around the globe, *Planet B-Boy* traces how b-boy culture has evolved from a Bronx-based activity into a global phenomenon. It focuses on b-boy crews from Korea, Japan, France, and the United States vying in the competition, providing viewers with a sense of how b-boys from all around the world negotiate their involvement with b-boy culture, what draws them to b-boying, and also the passion, commitment, and resilience that it takes to be a b-boy. Crews from Asia would dominate the competition that year, and the victories of the Japanese crew Ichigeki in Best Show and Choreography and the Korean crew Last For One in the overall competition would serve to further cement the idea of b-boying as an undeniably global expressive form.

An underlying theme conveyed in the film is the notion of b-boying as a unifying force among youth on a global scale. Notwithstanding the competition among the b-boy crews, a rhetoric of global unity permeates the film. According to the organizers of the Battle of the Year, the objective is for the competition to serve as a forum to promote b-boy culture and to foster unity and camaraderie among the various b-boy crews. As the legendary b-boy Ken Swift suggests toward the conclusion of the film, hip-hop has enabled youth in different parts of the globe to communicate regardless of their spoken language.[5] The implication here is that hip-hop constitutes a universal language that transcends national and linguistic differences.

The film presents the hip-hop nation as a particular kind of nation, a deterritorialized form that seems ideally suited for the current moment and ostensibly marked by the purported porousness of borders. The film articulates a particular vision of nationhood not predicated on a physical place or a one-to-one correspondence between a sense of belonging and a particular geographical location. In this articulation of nation, national boundaries are defined in social and affective terms rather than in geographic terms. In other words, social and affective ties supersede geographic ties in this particular vision of nation. The objective is not about the maintenance of boundaries but, rather, about transcending boundaries in the name of a global community. It is a vision of nation in which membership is not defined by birthright or legal status. Instead, the film articulates a vision of nationhood in which its constituency spans multiple national contexts, histories, and settings, all united by their love of and passion for b-boying.

The film, therefore, speaks to how hip-hop is best understood as a transnational expressive form. It foregrounds the way this expressive form shows a disregard for geographical boundaries and borders underlying conventional notions of nation and culture. The film draws attention to the contested nature of national boundaries and the instability of standard notions of belonging and nationhood. Instead, b-boys around the globe have cultivated modes of belonging and affiliation that run counter to territorially circumscribed understandings of belonging and affiliation. Ultimately, *Planet B-Boy* supports the assertion that the history and trajectory of hip-hop cannot be contained within nation-based narratives or accounted for in a linear fashion.

In many ways, hip-hop nation as articulated in the film does not quite fit the classic definition of a nation-state or exhibit many of the conventional markers that have come to be associated with the nation-state. Jared A. Ball's definition of hip-hop nation is relevant here in that the focal point is not necessarily what are considered conventional markers of the nation-state, such as political control of a geographical space. Instead, in Ball's view, a defining feature of hip-hop nation is a collective sense of recognition among members that they belong to the same nation.[6] This particular configuration very much resonates with the kind of nation valorized in the film.

The Continued Relevance of Nation

And yet, as the film also makes clear, "nation" continues to matter, as evidenced by the way the film is imbued with nationalist rhetoric and sentiments. For one thing, the competition was organized around the logic of the nation-state, with b-boy crews representing specific nations in what can be described as Olympic-style competition.[7] Echoing the Olympics, the Battle of the Year serves as a means for the competing b-boy crews to affirm their allegiance to and pride in their nation of origin. By the same token, the Battle of the Year constitutes a crucial site for the articulation of national aspirations and politics. There is also the use of national icons (such as the flag) in the film as a powerful way to convey a sense of pride and belonging to a particular nation. Last for One, the b-boy crew representative from Korea, provides a representative illustration of the nationalist tendencies that permeate the film. After hearing that they have been crowned champions of the competition, a member of the crew proudly hoists and waves the Korean flag along with an audience member. Members of Last for One, in other words, take a great deal of pride in achieving victory not just for their crew but also for Korea. Further reproducing the logic of nation, crews from particular nations have come to be known for cultivating a particular style (e.g. French b-boys for their intricate dancing, Korean b-boys for their power moves, and U.S. b-boys for their battle skills).

In the film, nationalist imperatives are displaced onto the familial and personal narratives of the various featured b-boy crews. Generational tensions in particular serve to accentuate the continued relevance of nation. B-boy Joe's father, for example, initially fails to understand and disapproves of his son's involvement in b-boying. After his son's crew wins the Battle of the Year competition, however, b-boy Joe's father comes to accept his son's involvement in b-boying, which in many ways signifies Korea's acceptance of b-boying as a legitimate art form. Recognition of b-boying as a legitimate art form is further signaled by Last For One's performances with the Seoul Traditional Orchestra and at the Seoul Arts Festival. The crew also made a commercial promoting Korean tourism. As one Korean b-boy puts it, "Once *our* dance has found its place in society it will help us make a living out of it. To make a living with what we love is the dream of all dancers" (emphasis added). Last For One's global notoriety coincides with and is concurrent with the crew's national acceptance. In effect, b-boy culture serves as vehicle whereby members of the crew negotiate their national status and ultimately attain recognition as legitimate national subjects and finally, national heroes.

Also striking in the film is the dominance of male b-boys, which is very much in concert with nationalist discourse in which men are accorded national agency and viewed as the ideal national representatives. As a number of feminist cultural critics put it, nation and gender are inextricably linked. In the words of Anne McClintock: "No nation in the world gives women and men the same access to the rights and resources of the nation-state."[8] She further makes the point that "women are typically constructed as the symbolic bearers of the nation but are denied any direct relation to national agency."[9] In keeping with the logic of nationalism, it would be the male b-boys, through their exploits and accomplishments, who would bring about the national acceptance of b-boying as a legitimate art form alongside what are considered "traditional" expressive forms of their nation of origin. The male b-boys, therefore, serve as catalysts for national progress, if progress is to be measured by the evolution of national cultural traditions and practices via the integration of "nontraditional" expressive forms.

Planet B-Boy, therefore, is tied to a nationalist framework and logic at the same time that it also speaks to the dynamics of globalization. Additionally, the film renders transparent the contradictions that seemingly abound in the deployment of "hip-hop nation." On one level, the global trafficking of hip-hop poses a challenge to the territorializing impulses and imperatives of the nation-state. Hip-hop, in other words, constitutes an expressive form that seemingly only makes sense in transnational terms. It seems incongruous, therefore, to deploy the trope of "nation" to refer to what has become an international phenomenon (and what some would argue has always been an international phenomenon). This has compelled Aniko Imre to make the following point: "In particular, there is something profoundly contradictory in the alliance between hip-hop and territorial nationalism. A migratory, hybrid musical form is employed to confirm primordial boundaries and blood ties."[10]

On another level, however, the film speaks to the complex dynamic between globalization and nationalism, a dynamic marked by a dialectical tension rather than opposition. Rouse describes the relationship this way: "As in many other areas, then, transnational has not so much displaced the national as resituated it and thus reworked its meanings."[11] The embrace of hip-hop, in other words, does not preclude an embrace of territorially based nationalism. Put another way, the film foregrounds how globalization and nationalism constitute mutually constitutive rather than mutually exclusive processes, inextricably linked processes rather than antagonistic ones. A number of cultural critics, for example, underscore the continued relevance of nationalism within the context of globalization, pointing to the bolstering of national ties in response to the purported homogeneous effects of globalization.[12] Within the realm of rap, for instance, MCs in different parts of the globe rely on hip-hop to augment nationalist claims.

Defining the Contours of the Hip-hop Nation

What constitutes the border of the "hip-hop nation" is very much a contested issue, an issue that *Planet B-Boy* does not directly address in its seamless representation of what constitutes this nation. This is evident in the various views held by cultural critics about the contours of the hip-hop nation. Cultural critics like Neil Strauss, for example, subscribe to an expansive notion of the hip-hop nation, conceiving of it as a nation that overlaps with other ones. One of these nations is the one that Strauss himself admittedly inhabits, what he refers to as Gray, a nation in which "the boundaries are more fluid and blurry than many people would like to believe: white people are listening to and using elements of rap not for theft but because they relate to it, because the music is a legitimate part of their cultural heritage."[13] He goes on to say that "in this world, black rappers are finding that it is now possible to serve both the black and white audience without betraying either."[14] He then provides other examples of nations that overlap with the hip-hop nation, including the nations of Latin America and Asian America. Toward the end of the article, Strauss poses the question of who owns hip-hop, providing a list of the diverse constituency of hip-hop and asserting that hip-hop belongs to everyone because of the way it speaks to a diverse constituency. He concludes: "This, at the dawn of a new millennium, is the hip-hop empire: an aggregation of many nations, under God, very divisible, with rhymes and beats for all."[15]

Similarly, other cultural critics subscribe to a broad definition of hip-hop nation but do so according to different terms. Rather then conceive of hip-hop as comprising overlapping nations, for example, Ian Maxwell emphasizes the transnational dimensions of the hip-hop nation. Accordingly, he defines hip-hop nation as

> a transnational entity manifested, in this antipodean context, in the absence of an existential shared grounding of participants in race, class, or physical

proximity (either to each other, in terms of a 'hood, or to their brothers over oceans), means a commitment in the first instance to the three key hip-hop practices—rapping, writing, and breaking—and to something variously referred to as the "essence," the "ideology," the "hard core," or the truth of hip-hop, a truth that . . . could be found in the affective thrall of the music itself.[16]

For Maxwell, then, what matters as the underlying basis of the hip-hop nation is one's "commitment" to what are the constituent elements of hip-hop that serves to legitimize one's involvement regardless of one's proximity to the purported origins of hip-hop or, in his words, "the absence of an existential shared grounding of participants."

Similarly, Aniko Imre emphasizes the transnational dimensions of the hip-hop nation: "Hip-hop, then, provides a virtual home of shared experiences, a space of connectedness and belonging to a transnational community often called 'hip-hop nation.'"[17] Relying on Benedict Anderson's notion of imagined community, R. Scott Heath makes a similar point about the transnational scope of hip-hop even as it is conceived in terms of a "nation." He makes the point that "as a model of community organization, this 'nation' of hip-hop is necessarily figurative in that the consolidated group of cultural producers and consumers would be recognized as *inter*national and *trans*national in terms of nation proper."[18]

For Rachel Devitt, "migration," "dispersal," and "pastiche" are constitutive features of hip-hop from the outset to the extent that hip-hop cannot be contained within the discourse and logic of nation: "Hip-hop's origins in migration and dispersal and its insistence on pastiche, on borrowing from multiple, overlapping sources, cutting them all up, and then pasting everything together again on a complex community bulletin board of signs and signifiers that disrupts dominant semiotics, constantly recreate the genre as an always diasporic art form, able to move faster than a speeding mp3, to leap nation-state constructs in a single bound."[19] By the same token, Halifu Osumare deploys the term "hip-hop globe" as a frame to signify hip-hop's global articulations. He makes the point that "if U.S. rap is black Americans' CNN, then global rap could become the BBC of youths worldwide."[20] And in her consideration of West Indian youth, Oneka LaBennett speaks of both a hip-hop nation and a global hip-hop planet.[21]

The cultural critic Toure also provides an expansive definition of what constitutes the hip-hop nation. Comparing the hip-hop nation with more conventional notions of nation, he asserts that hip-hop constitutes "a place with its own language, culture, and history. It is as much a nation as Italy or

Zambia. A place my countrymen call the Hip-Hop Nation, purposefully in-voking all of the jingoistic pride that nationalists throughout history have leaned on."[22] He goes on to make the point that it "exists in any place where hip-hop music is being played or hip-hop attitude is being exuded."[23]

In contrast to the foregoing cultural critics, however, Toure qualifies his definition of what constitutes the hip-hop nation in more delimited ways. More specifically, he is quick to assert that black men are at the forefront of the cul-ture and should remain so, given the history and legacy of white supremacy even while acknowledging hip-hop's multiracial origins and influences: "The Nation's pioneers were a multiracial bunch—whites were among the early elite graffiti artists and Latinos were integral to the shaping of DJing and MCing, b-boying, and general hip-hop style. Today's nation makes brothers of men black, brown, yellow, and white. But this world was built to worship urban black maleness: the way we speak, walk, dance, dress, think. We are revered by others, but our leadership is and will remain black. As it should."[24] In contrast to cultural critics like Strauss, then, Toure provides a definition of the hip-hop nation tied to blackness in a way that delineates the stakes for black men.

Likewise, Cheryl L. Keyes provides an all-encompassing definition of hip-hop nation but with the following qualification. For Keyes, "the Hip-Hop Nation comprises a community of artists and adherents who espouse street performance aesthetics as expressed through the four elements of hip-hop."[25] She goes on to say that "although the Hip-Hop Nation embraces anyone who performs any of its artistic forms, a follower or member of the Zulu Nation, the philosophy that undergirds its belief is guided by black national and street consciousness."[26] In her conceptualization of hip-hop nation, Keyes grounds her definition within the context of black nationalist ideology and culture, and akin to Toure, she does not view this notion of hip-hop nation as mutu-ally exclusive from an inclusive notion of hip-hop nation.

For H. Samy Alim, language is the crucial component that serves as the constitutive basis of the hip-hop nation. Speaking primarily of rap, he posits a direct connection among language, identity, and nation, defining the hip-hop nation primarily in linguistic terms: "HHNL [hip hop nation language] is central to the identity and act of envisioning an entity known as the HHN [hip hop nation]."[27] He foregrounds what he describes as the significance of a "cultural specific 'code of communication' that allows the various Hip-hop communities that comprise the HHN to stay in contact."[28] In Alim's view, the hip-hop nation is very much grounded in AAL (African American language) and street vernacular, and more broadly, African American oral traditions and practices. For Alim, hip-hop vernacular is synonymous with African American vernacular.

Other hip-hop scholars are more interested in the deployment of black nationalism within rap music, particularly during the so-called Golden Era of hip-hop, than in specifying its borders in certain terms. Jeffrey Louis Decker, for instance, locates the hip-hop nation within the context of the legacy and trajectory of black nationalism. He draws a connection between nation-conscious MCs and the black power movement of the 1960s and Afro-centric thought. Decker then proceeds to identify the two primary strains of hip-hop nationalism, what he describes as "sixties-inspired hip-hop nationalism" and "Afrocentric hip-hop nationalism." He views "hip-hop nationalists as organic *cultural* intellectuals to the degree that their activities are directly linked to the everyday struggles of black folk and that their music critically engages the popular knowledge of which they are a part."[29] Decker goes on to discuss the appeal and function of nation: "The language of nation is appropriated by the hip-hop community as a vehicle for contesting the changing discursive and institutional structures of racism in America."[30] Echoing Anderson's work, he is less concerned with judging the truth (accuracy or inaccuracy) of any particular historical claim made by hip-hop nationalism than in attempting to describe and interpret the logic behind its deployment of nationalist discourse.

Similar to Decker, Charise L. Cheney's project locates rap nationalism within the larger trajectory of black nationalism through a consideration of a cohort of MCs she describes as raptivists. She deploys hip-hop nation "to refer to a cohort of black neonationalist rap artists," while acknowledging how the term has come to be used to refer "to hip-hop artists and fans regardless of their political standpoint."[31] Forging a link between hip-hop nationalism and black nationalism, Cheney asserts that raptivism constitutes a form of black neonationalism and more specifically, contemporary articulations of black nationalism.

What is distinct about Decker's and Cheney's analyses is the reflexiveness in their works, particularly around issues of gender and sexuality, a reflexiveness sorely lacking in many contemporary accounts. According to Decker, for instance, a challenge for hip-hop nationalism is its inability and unwillingness to critically address black nationalism's retrograde tendencies. A problem plaguing hip-hop nationalism is its uncritical embrace of the masculinist logic of black nationalism, which serves to sanction the objectification of women. As Decker puts it, "black women are either good or bad, mothers or whores, wives or gold-digging lovers."[32] Cautioning against the tendency to romanticize black revolutionary politics or to uncritically conflate the distinct and often opposing agendas of militant black organizations, Decker foregrounds the limits of hip-hop nationalism as a vehicle for the liberation of black women.

For Cheney, the liberatory potential of rap nationalism has been compromised by its regressive gender and sexual politics. Rap nationalism, like black nationalism, has been primarily concerned with the liberation of black heterosexual men. In her view, its promotion of notions of collective self-consciousness and self-determination is informed by a gendered ideology and discourse that serves to recoup and reclaim black manhood at the expense of nonblack heterosexual men. "Liberation" and "empowerment" within this discourse is very much tied to a hegemonic masculinity that, in Cheney's words, "suppresses the heterogeneity of experiences in African America."[33] More recently, Oneka LaBennett has provided a gendered analysis of West Indian female youth involvement in hip-hop. Building on the Marcyliena Morgan's use of citizenship in her consideration of the hip-hop underground scene in Los Angeles, LaBennett makes the point that the pursuit of dual citizenship is a vexed and shaky proposition for West Indian female youth.[34]

Notwithstanding the currency of the trope of nation, its invocation has been marked, with few exceptions, by a lack of critical self-reflexiveness, raising a number of questions that have yet to be adequately considered. Appeals to and the referential deployment of nation, for example, have theoretical and political implications, and yet these implications remain unelaborated and uninterrogated. R. Scott Heath is one of the few cultural critics to raise the issue of what it means to conceive of hip-hop in terms of a nation, bringing up an important question: "Who sets the definitive parameters of a particular culture and who chooses the representations of this culture?"[35] He goes on to make the point that

> though the hip-hop community has been depicted as a cohesive nationalist entity, its nationhood is at best a shaky postulation in that a consistent definition of the parameters of this community and the specific criteria for the constitution of its supposed citizenship remain missing. Hip-hop might be, at this point, better understood as a site of convergence of many highly variegated communities, and its history, a text being written from an array of different perspectives and conceptual localities. Particularly in the last few years, more hip-hop practitioners have shown tendencies toward a conscious cosmopolitanism, redefining the potential readership to acknowledge hip-hop's multigenerational, multinational, and multilingual character, and further indicating some of the significant ways in which nationhood has been taken for granted.[36]

Here Heath raises a number of crucial points including what constitutes the criteria for citizenship within the hip-hop nation. Given hip-hop's varied constituencies and trajectories, he posits that it is no longer tenable to conceive of hip-hop as "a single, homogeneous hip-hop nation."[37] Instead, Heath emphasizes how the hip-hop nation encompasses a multiplicity of converging communities on a global scale.

Heath's formulation, however, begs the following questions: What, then, constitute the bounds of the hip-hop nation (and who gets to define it)? How do we conceive of the involvement of what Heath describes as "variegated communities"? How do we account for "hip-hop's multigenerational, multinational, and multilingual character"? What would be considered fault lines and fissures in this so-called hip-hop nation? Why the trope of nation, especially given hip-hop's status as a global expressive form? Why the deployment of "nation," given the highly problematic status of nationalist discourse and logic?

As currently constituted, hip-hop nation serves to reproduce problematic aspects of nationalist discourse and logic, namely patriarchal and heteronormative logic and discourse. Overlooked in contemporary usage of the trope of nation, for instance, is a body of feminist cultural criticism that has launched powerful and compelling critiques of the complicity of nationalist discourses with gender hierarchies. Feminist cultural critics, including Anne McClintock, Aamir Mufti, and Ella Shohat, underscore the ways women have had a problematic relationship to the nation. These cultural critics point to how familial and domestic metaphors mark and position women's bodies in very particular ways, as crucial to the reproduction of the nation and the maintenance of its boundaries.[38] Also overlooked is queer theory's critique of the ways heterosexuality is fundamental to the way in which the nation imagines itself. The nation, in other words, is imagined in a heterosexist manner in which nonheterosexuals are excluded from the terms of national belonging and "good" citizenship. Hip-hop, in other words, has been unable to extricate itself from problematic aspects of nationalist ideology and discourse through its deployment of nation as an unmarked formation.[39]

In the next section, I rely on the works of a select number of Filipino cultural critics engaged in a critical analysis of Filipino American cultural productions. While not specifically addressing the problematics of hip-hop nation (or hip-hop for that matter), their focus on Filipino American cultural productions serves to contextualize my own work. I am particularly interested in how DJing fits in relation to the wide array of cultural forms and practices that comprise the terrain of Filipino popular culture. I find especially useful their critical inquiry into how nation is implicated in a wide array of Filipino American cultural productions in vexed and complicated ways. These cultural critics gesture provocatively toward the kind of analysis that does not rely on a multi-cultural framework and logic, thereby suggesting how we might think about Filipino American cultural productions in ways that do not lose sight of the imbrication among U.S., Filipino, and hip-hop national formations.

Filipinos and the Vexed Status of Nation

In *Suspended Apocalypse*, Dylan Rodriguez speaks of an emergent post-1965 Filipino Americanism as a particular kind of nation-building project that he characterizes as "deformed." Here Rodriguez is alluding to "the peculiarity and historical specificity of Filipino Americanism as an expression of allegiance with the local and global political logics of the contemporary U.S. nation-building project within which the Filipino American communion is a minor component."[40] Filipino Americanism, in other words, is very much in collusion with white supremacist logic that is at the foundation of U.S. nation building.

Sarita See speaks of a cohort of artists constitutive of an emergent "Filipino American cultural moment," marked by what she describes as practices of decolonization. Emphasizing the performative and the theatrical, she looks to the works of these artists as providing a potentially important rubric for reconsidering the workings of both empire and nation. These artists deploy the body in a way that provides a counter to national mythologies, such as narratives of immigrant assimilation. She interrogates the works of such artists as the comedian Rex Navarrete and his reappropriation of language, and the visual artist Reanne Estrada and her resignification of degradable materials.[41]

Also focusing on the performative and the corporeal, Theodore S. Gonzalves looks to Pilipino Cultural Night (PCN) as a vehicle for staging national identity and culture and in the process, for refashioning the parameters of Filipino Americanness. He makes the point that "at a collective level, the choreography reminds viewers of how a nation may be expressed as a community in motion—directed, purposeful, disciplined, commensurable with the stagecraft of other nations, and, ultimately, answerable to the invented body politics."[42] Gonzalves considers Filipino American participation—especially college-aged Filipino Americans—in this expressive form as part of efforts by this cohort to reenvision time and space, to provide a counter to state-sponsored narratives such as the narrative of immigrant assimilation.

The foregoing speaks to the ways Filipino American culture constitutes a vexed and complicated terrain as well as to the varied nature of Filipino American cultural politics. Most relevant for this study, however, is the way the aforementioned works underscore the ways Filipino American cultural productions constitute an engagement with nation that is neither simple nor straightforward. What is significant about these works is the way they point tentatively to critical pathways for scrutinizing the ways Filipino American cultural productions serve to both reinscribe and disrupt normative mythologies, assumptions, and tropes of nation.

In the case of Filipino DJs, their unparalleled exploits seem to have secured their place within the hip-hop nation. Their contributions to one of the pillars of hip-hop seem to have established their hip-hop credentials beyond doubt. In the film *Scratch*, for example, Cut Chemist pays ISP the ultimate compliment, asserting that he considers the primarily all-Filipino crew the best DJ crew of all time.[43] As I have suggested earlier, however, Filipino DJs engage in the kind of deraced politics that Rodriguez has described in another context as complicit with U.S. multicultural discourse and logic. Cut Chemist's compliment, for instance, very much echoes a contributionist approach that leaves in place the foundational logic and discourse of nation. While Filipino youth involvement in DJing has served to expand the grounds from which to consider the bounds of Filipinoness, it has also served to perpetuate narrow notions of nationalist discourse and logic.

In providing a brief consideration of Filipino youth involvement in DJing in relation to other Filipino American expressive forms, I have endeavored to open up a critical space to scrutinize questions of cultural ownership and entitlement and, in this conclusion, cultural belonging. To borrow from Heath, while "the time for speaking of a single, homogeneous hip_hop nation may have passed,"[44] so too speaking of hip-hop (and hip-hop nation) in an unmarked fashion, abstracted from the workings of power and history. To continue to do so fails to substantively grapple with the contours and trajectory of racial formations and discourses in the post–civil rights era.

Notes

Introduction

1. The ITF is an organization that began sponsoring DJ competitions worldwide in 1996; it promotes the notion that the turntable is an instrument that produces rather than just plays music. Scratching and beat juggling are common DJ techniques and have become standards of battling. Doc Rice, a DJ himself, describes scratching this way: "Virtually all scratches involve moving the record by hand in a forward and backward manner" and "require the use of the fader" (Doc Rice, "Essential DJ Fundamentals: The Language of Scratching," *Rap Pages*, September 1998, 30). Beat juggling, on the other hand, involves creating "a new rhythm without cross-fader use by pausing both records alternately—one hand for each record—and breaking down the beat and separating the drum elements." Finally, team or DJ bands refers to DJs performing as a team, "with each member taking on the role of separate musicians, such as vocals, drums, etc., and switching off between them" (Doc Rice, "Essential DJ Fundamentals, Part 2: Tricks of the Trade," *Rap Pages*, October 1998, 40).

2. For example, the 1998 DMC National Champion from Australia, DJ Dexter, and the 1998 DMC National Champion from Canada, Lil' Jazz, are both of Filipino descent.

3. The claiming of an expressive form not considered Filipino is not specific to DJing, as Filipino youth have made similar claims with regards to Latin freestyle, house, and R&B. Elizabeth H. Pisares also notes that these claims are geographically specific. Italian and Greek Americans on the East Coast, for example, consider freestyle music as their own, while Filipinos in California claim it as theirs. See Elizabeth M. Pisares, "Do You Mis(recognize) Me: Jocelyn Enriquez, Filipina/o Invisibility, and the Condition of Perpetual Absence," in *Positively No Filipinos Allowed: Building Communities and Discourse*, ed. Antonio T. Tiongson Jr., Ed Gutierrez, and Ric Gutierrez, 172–98 (Philadelphia: Temple University Press, 2006).

4. Conventional markers of Filipinoness include language (fluency in Tagalog or other Filipino dialects), so-called indigenous dances (knowing how to do these dances), and food (incorporation of Filipino food in one's diet).

5. Allan Punzalan Isaac, *American Tropics: Articulating Filipino America* (Minneapolis: University of Minnesota Press, 2006), xxv.

6. Jonathan Y. Okamura, *Imagining the Filipino American Diaspora: Transnational Relations, Identities, and Communities* (New York: Garland Publishing, Inc., 1998).

7. S. Craig Watkins, *Hip-hop Matters: Politics, Pop Culture, and the Struggle for the Soul of the Movement* (Boston: Beacon Press, 2004), 150.

8. Juan Flores, "Puerto Rican and Proud, Boyee! Rap, Roots and Amnesia," in *Microphone Fiends: Youth Music and Youth Culture*, ed. Andrew Ross and Tricia Rose (New York: Routledge, 1994), 95.

9. Jacqueline Urla, "'We Are All Malcolm X!': Negu Gorriak, Hip-hop, and the Basque Political Imaginary," in *Global Noise: Rap and Hip-hop outside the U.S.A.*, ed. Tony Mitchell (Middletown: Wesleyan University Press, 2001), 173–74 .

10. Virginia R. Dominguez, "Invoking Culture: The Messy Side of 'Cultural Politics,'" *South Atlantic Quarterly* 91, no. 1 (1992): 22.

11. R. Scott Heath, "True Heads: Historicizing the Hip_Hop 'Nation' in Context," *Callaloo* 29, no. 3 (2006): 846.

12. Shu-Mei Shih, "Comparative Racialization: An Introduction," *PMLA* 123, no. 5 (2008): 1350.

13. See, for example, essay contributions to Heike Raphael-Hernandez and Shannon Steen, eds. *AfroAsian Encounters: Culture, History, Politics* (New York: New York University Press, 2006).

14. Scott Kurashige, *The Shifting Grounds of Race: Black and Japanese Americans in the Making of Multiethnic Los Angeles* (Princeton: Princeton University Press, 2008), 288; Grace Hong, "Strange Affinities," *CSW Update Newsletter*, 7.

15. Ella Shohat, "Area Studies, Gender Studies, and the Cartographies of Knowledge," *Social Text* 20, no. 3 (2002): 67–78.

16. Helen H. Jun's focus is nineteenth-century black press engagement with Orientalist discourse as a means to grapple with the complications attached to African American citizenship. See Jun, "Black Orientalism: Nineteenth-Century Narratives of Race and U.S. Citizenship," *American Quarterly* 58, no. 4 (2006): 1051.

17. Alexander G. Weheliye, *Phonographies: Grooves in Sonic Afro-Modernity* (Durham: Duke University Press, 2005); Paul Gilroy, *The Black Atlantic: Modernity and Double Consciousness* (Cambridge, Mass.: Harvard University Press, 1993).

18. Lok Siu, "Queen of the Chinese Colony: Gender, Nation, and Belonging in Diaspora," *Anthropological Quarterly* 78, no. 3 (2005): 511–42; Jacqueline Nassy Brown, "Black Liverpool, Black America and the Gendering of Diasporic Space," *Cultural Anthropology* 13, no. 3 (1998): 291–325; Gayatri Gopinath, "'Bombay, U.K., Yuba City': Bhangra Music and the Engendering of Diaspora," *Diaspora* 4, no. 3 (1995): 303–21.

19. Neda Maghbouleh, "'Inherited Nostalgia' among Second-Generation Iranian Americans: A Case Study of a Southern California University," *Journal of Intercultural Studies* 31, no. 2 (2010): 199–218; Victoria Mason, "Children of the 'Idea of Palestine': Negotiating Identity, Belonging and Home in the Palestinian Diaspora," *Journal of Intercultural Studies* 28, no. 3 (2007): 271–85; Nedim Karakayali, "Duality and Diversity in the Lives of Immigrant Children: Rethinking the "Problem of the Second Generation"

in Light of Immigrant Autobiographies," *Canadian Review of Sociology and Anthropology* 42, no. 3 (2005): 325–43.

20. See, for example, Jigna Desai, "Planet Bollywood: Indian Cinema Abroad," in *East Main Street: Asian American Popular Culture*, ed. Shilpa Dave, Leilani Nishime, Tasha G. Oren, and Robert G. Lee, 55–71 (New York: New York University Press, 2005).

21. For a consideration of how both first- and second-generation Filipinos grapple with questions of national belonging, see Benito M. Vergara Jr., *Pinoy Capital: The Filipino Nation in Daly City* (Philadelphia: Temple University Press, 2008). See also Dylan Rodriguez, *Suspended Apocalypse: White Supremacy, Genocide, and the Filipino Condition* (Minneapolis: University of Minnesota Press, 2010); Sarita Echavez See, *Decolonized Eye: Filipino Art and Performance* (Minneapolis: University of Minnesota Press, 2009); and Theodore Gonzalves, *The Day the Dancers Stayed: Performing in the Filipino/American Diaspora* (Philadelphia: Temple University Press, 2009).

22. Nitasha Tamar Sharma, *Hip-hop Desis: South Asian Americans, Blackness, and a Global Race Consciousness* (Durham: Duke University Press, 2010); Anthony Kwame Harrison, *Hip-hop Underground: The Integrity and Ethics of Racial Identification* (Philadelphia: Temple University Press, 2009). As Inez H. Templeton notes, this remains a lacunae in hip-hop studies scholarship, the absence of studies based on a direct engagement with members of the hip-hop community. Instead, the bulk of the research relies on methodology that Templeton describes as reminiscent of Hebdige's work on subcultures. See Templeton, "Where in the World Is the Hip-hop Nation?" *Popular Music* 22, no. 2 (2003): 241–45.

23. Heath, "True Heads," 862–63.

24. Ibid., 864.

25. Ibid.

26. R. Scott Heath, "Hip_hop Now: An Introduction," *Callaloo* 29, no. 3 (2006): 715.

27. *Scratch*, directed by Doug Pray (New York: Palm Pictures, 2001), DVD.

28. Isaac, *American Tropics*, 178.

1. The African Americanization of Hip-hop

1. See, e.g., Mickey Hess, *Is Hip-hop Dead?: The Past, Present, and Future of America's Most Wanted Music* (Westport, Conn.: Praeger, 2007); Jeffrey O. G. Ogbar, Hip-Hop Revolution: The Culture and Politics of Rap (Lawrence: University Press of Kansas, 2007).

2. See, for example, *Hip-hop: Beyond Beats and Rhymes*, directed by Byron Hurt (Northampton, Mass.: Media Education Foundation, 2006), DVD, which provides a critical examination of the gender and sexual politics of hip-hop and in particular, the way it has served as a vehicle for the perpetuation of hypermasculinist images of black men. See also T. Denean Sharpley-Whiting, *Pimps Up, Ho's Down: Hip-hop's Hold on Young Black Women* (New York: New York University Press, 2007); Gwendolyn D. Pough, *Check It While I Wreck It: Black Womanhood, Hip-hop Culture, and the Public Sphere* (Boston: Northeastern University Press, 2004).

3. Harrison, *Hip-hop Underground*, 83.

4. Templeton, "Where in the World Is the Hip-hop Nation?," 241.

5. Watkins, *Hip-hop Matters*, 150.

6. Bakari Kitwana, *Why White Kids Love Hip-hop; Wankstas, Wiggers, Wannabes, and the New Reality of Race in America* (New York: Basic Civitas Books, 2005), 150. See also Imani Perry, *Prophets of the Hood: Politics and Poetics in Hip-hop* (Durham: Duke University Press, 2005), and John F. Szwed, "The Real Old School," in *The Vibe History of Hip-hop*, ed. Alan Light, 3–12 (New York: Three Rivers Press, 1999), who both subscribe to a similar point of view as Bakari Kitwana.

7. Steven Hager, *Hip-hop: The Illustrated History of Break Dancing, Rap Music, and Graffiti* (New York: St. Martin's Press, 1984).

8. Although Dwyer's focus is on the assumptions underlying the historiography of the civil rights movement, his analysis and critique has a great deal of relevance to the historiography of hip-hop. See Owen J. Dwyer, "Interpreting the Civil Rights Movement: Place, Memory, and Conflict," *Professional Geographer* 52, no. 4 (2000): 663.

9. Hager, *Hip-hop*, 68.

10. Ibid.

11. Ibid.

12. Ibid., 70.

13. Ibid., 44.

14. David Toop, *The Rap Attack: African Jive to New York Hip-hop* (Boston: South End Press, 1984), 115.

15. Ibid., 32.

16. Nelson George, Sally Banes, Susan Flinker, and Patty Romanowski, *Fresh: Hip-hop Don't Stop* (New York: Sarah Lazin Books, 1985), 13.

17. Ibid., 26.

18. Toop, *The Rap Attack*, 18–19.

19. Hager, *Hip-hop*, chap. 6.

20. Vee Bravo, senior editor of *Stress* magazine, quoted in Raquel Z. Rivera, *New York Ricans from the Hip-hop Zone* (New York: Palgrave Macmillan, 2003), 51.

21. Ibid., 50–51.

22. Joseph G. Schloss, *Foundation: B-boys, B-girls, and Hip-hop Culture in New York* (Oxford: Oxford University Press, 2009).

23. Phrase taken from Flores, "Puerto Rican and Proud," 97.

24. Juan Flores, *From Bomba to Hip-hop: Puerto Rican Culture and Latino Identity* (New York: Columbia University Press, 2000), 92.

25. Ibid., 90.

26. Rivera, *New York Ricans*, 8–9.

27. Ibid., x.

28. Ibid., 42.

29. Gilroy, *The Black Atlantic*, 2.

30. Ibid. See also Paul Gilroy, *Small Acts: Thoughts on the Politics of Black Cultures* (New York: Serpent's Tail, 1993).

31. Gilroy, *The Black Atlantic*, esp. chap. 3.

32. Ibid.

33. See, for example, Ian Condry, *Hip-hop Japan: Rap and the Paths of Cultural Globalization* (Durham: Duke University Press, 2006). He aims to shed light on the imbrication between the global and Japan—what this reveals about the variegated articulations of globalization processes. At the same time, he aims to complicate Japanese youth engagement with hip-hop, drawing attention to the ways Japanese youth take up hip-hop rather than focusing on whether or not Japanese youth can articulate an understanding of race and hip-hop. He is particularly interested in how Japanese youth involvement within hip-hop can serve as a vehicle for the discussion of race and racial differences as well as a vehicle for forging transracial alliances.

34. Tony Mitchell, "Introduction: Another Root—Hip-hop outside the U.S.A.," in *Global Noise: Rap and Hip-hop outside the U.S.A.*, ed. Tony Mitchell (Middletown: Wesleyan University Press, 2001), 4.

35. Ibid., 10. See also Andy Bennett, who in *Popular Music and Youth Culture: Music, Identity and Place* (New York: St. Martin's Press, 2000) focuses on local inscriptions of hip-hop and in particular, rearticulations of meanings in ways that is inextricably bound up with local experience. He is particularly concerned with how music is taken up in the context of the daily lives of young people.

36. Mitchell, "Introduction," 1–2.

37. Urla, "'We Are All Malcolm X!,'" 173.

38. Robin D. G. Kelley, foreword to *The Vinyl Ain't Final: Hip-hop and the Globalization of Black Popular Culture*, ed. Dipannita Basu and Sidney J. Lemelle (Ann Arbor: Pluto Press, 2006), xi.

39. Perry, *Prophets of the Hood*, 10.

40. Ibid., 12.

41. Ibid.

42. Robin D. G. Kelley, *Yo' Mama's Disfunktional! Fighting the Culture Wars in Urban America* (Boston: Beacon Press, 1997), 42.

43. Szwed, "The Real Old School," 7.

44. Kitwana, *Why White Kids Love Hip-hop*, 150.

45. Ibid.

46. Condry, *Hip-hop Japan*, 24.

47. Dipannita Basu and Sidney J. Lemelle, introduction to *The Vinyl Ain't Final*, 1–15.

48. Marc D. Perry, "Global Black Self-Fashionings: Hip-hop as Diasporic Space," *Identities: Global Studies in Culture and Power* 15 (2008): 635.

49. Ibid., 636.

50. Sharma, *Hip-hop Desis*, 2.

51. Ibid., 215.

52. Ibid., 215–16.

53. Ibid., 217.

54. Harrison, *Hip-hop Underground*, 45.

55. Ibid., 119.

56. S. Watkins, *Hip-hop Matters*, 150.

2. The Racialization of DJ Culture

1. See Rivera, *New York Ricans*.

2. See, for example, ibid.; Ivor L. Miller, *Aerosol Kingdom: Subway Painters of New York City* (Jackson: University Press of Mississippi, 2002).

3. Rivera, *New York Ricans*, 58.

4. Ibid., 61.

5. Schloss, *Foundation*.

6. Rivera, *New York Ricans*, chap. 4.

7. H. Samy Alim, "Hip-hop Nation Language," in *Language in the USA: Themes for the Twenty-First Century*, ed. Edward Finegan and John R. Rickford (Cambridge: Cambridge University Press, 2004), 393.

8. Rivera, *New York Ricans*.

9. Quoted in Lakandiwa M. de Leon, "Filipinotown and the DJ Scene: Cultural Expression and Identity Affirmation of Filipino American Youth in Los Angeles," in *Asian American Youth: Culture, Identity, and Ethnicity*, ed. Jennifer Lee and Min Zhou (New York: Routledge, 2004), 197. While this explanation holds some merit, it does not adequately account for the dominance of Filipinos in DJing. It may well be the case that hip-hop's racialized discourses compel nonblack participants to carve out niches in DJing, writing, or b-boying, but it does not explain the high concentration of DJs among Filipinos. In other words, it should just be as easy for Filipino youth to establish themselves in those elements of hip-hop not narrowly identified as black, yet Filipino youth are particularly attracted to DJing. The high concentration of DJs among Filipinos, therefore, is not simply a function of the narrow identification of MCing with blackness. Instead, it is attributable to a serendipitous confluence of circumstances, including Filipino youth involvement in the DJ mobile scene, which put them in a position to play a key role in the resurgence of DJing.

10. Rivera, *New York Ricans*, 100.

11. In both academic and popular texts, there is now recognition of the significance of Latinos, namely Puerto Rican youth, to the emergence and evolution of hip-hop. Rivera, for instance, points to the widespread recognition of the pivotal role of Latinos, along with blacks, in the emergence and evolution of hip-hop in popular media, including hip-hop magazines like *The Source* and rap video shows like *Rap City*, and in the academic literature, such as works by Christopher Holmes Smith and Peter McLaren. She goes on to say, however, that notwithstanding this recognition, the specificity of Latinos continues to be underspecified in these accounts. See Rivera, *New York Ricans*.

12. Rivera, *New York Ricans*, chap. 5. See also Ogbar, *Hip-hop Revolution*.

13. Jason Tanz, *Other People's Property: A Shadow History of Hip-hop in White America* (New York: Bloomsbury, 2007), 157.

14. Tanz, *Other People's Property*; Harrison, *Hip-hop Underground*. There is now a growing literature on the evolving status of white MCs within hip-hop, with a particular focus on Eminem. See, for example, Liam Grealy, "Negotiating Cultural Authenticity in Hip-hop: Mimicry, Whiteness, and Eminem," *Continuum: Journal of Media and Cultural Studies* 22, no. 6 (2008): 851–65; and Mickey Hess, "Hip-hop Realness and the White Performer," *Critical Studies in Media Communication* 22, no. 5 (2005): 372–89.

15. Craig Castleman, *Getting Up: Subway Graffiti in New York* (Cambridge, Mass.: MIT Press, 1982), 67.

16. Joe Austin, "Knowing Their Place: Local Knowledge, Social Prestige, and the Writing Formation in New York City," in *Generations of Youth: Youth Cultures and History in Twentieth-Century America*, ed. Joe Austin and Michael Nevin Willard (New York: New York University Press, 1998), 241.

17. Jeff Chang, *Can't Stop, Won't Stop: A History of the Hip-hop Generation* (New York: St. Martin's Press, 2005), 119.

18. Gregory J. Snyder, *Graffiti Lives: Beyond the Tag in New York's Urban Underground* (New York: New York University Press, 2009), 29.

19. *Style Wars*, directed by Tony Silver (Los Angeles: Public Art Films, 1983), DVD.

20. Hager, *Hip-hop*.

21. Snyder, *Graffiti Lives*, 2–3.

22. Miller notes that in many ways, this was a function of imperatives of writing culture—that is, crews made it easier to navigate the urban landscape of New York and made it easier for writers to put up their art. See Miller, *Aerosol Kingdom*, esp. his discussion of multiethnic crews, 29–33. See also Joe Austin, *Taking the Train: How Graffiti Art Became an Urban Crisis in New York City* (New York: Columbia University Press, 2001).

23. Ibid., 29.

24. Ibid., 31.

25. Austin, "Knowing Their Place," 244. See also Austin, *Taking the Train*.

26. Snyder, *Graffiti Lives*, 5.

27. Quoted in Miller, *Aerosol Kingdom*, 31.

28. Ibid., 30.

29. Ibid., 17.

30. Ibid., 165.

31. Ibid., 17.

32. Hager, *Hip-hop*, 83.

33. Trac 2, quoted in Chang, *Can't Stop, Won't Stop*, 117.

34. Rivera, *New York Ricans*, 75.

35. Ibid., 75.

36. Schloss, *Foundation*, 16.

37. Ibid., 38.

38. This is foregrounded, for example, in the film *The Freshest Kids: A History of the B-Boy*, directed by Israel (Chatsworth, Calif.: Image Entertainment, 2002), DVD.

39. Quoted in Cristina Veran, "Breaking It All Down: The Rise and Fall and Rise of the B-Boy Kingdom," in *The Vibe History of Hip-hop*, ed. Alan Light (New York: Three Rivers Press, 1999), 59.

40. Ibid., 57.

41. Ibid., 59.

42. Rivera, *New York Ricans*, 67–77.

43. See, for example, Luke Crisell, Phil White, and Rob Principe, *On the Record: The Scratch DJ Academy Guide* (New York: St. Martin's Press, 2009).

44. Ulf Poschardt, *DJ Culture*, trans. Shaun Whiteside (London: Quartet Books, 2000).

45. Crisell, White, and Principe, *On the Record*, 2–3.

46. Ibid., 3.

47. Ibid., 142.

48. Kurt B. Reighley, *Looking for the Perfect Beat: The Art and Culture of the DJ* (New York: MTV Books, 2000), 176.

49. Billy Jam, "Bay Area Part II," *Strength*, no. 10 (n.d.), http://www.solesides .com/winblad/bayareastrength10.html.

50. Ibid.

51. Additionally, the Bay Area has come to be known for its hip-hop activism, laying claim to what is generally considered the most sophisticated hip-hop activist infrastructure in the nation.

52. Harrison, *Hip-hop Underground*, 7.

53. Ibid., 11–12.

54. Ibid., 13.

55. Neva Chonin, quoted in Liz Lufkin, "Hip-hop Breakthrough," *San Francisco Chronicle*, November 1, 1998, http://www.sfgate.com/entertainment/article/Hip-Hop -Breakthrough-2980909.php.

56. *Scratch*.

57. Rachel Devitt, "Lost in Translation: Filipino Diaspora(s), Postcolonial Hip-hop, and the Problems of Keeping It Real for the 'Contentless' Black Eyed Peas," *Asian Music* 39, no. 1 (Winter/Spring 2008): 120.

58. Ibid., 119.

59. Quoted in Marty Mapes, "Interview with Doug Pray," Movie Habit, April 12, 2002, http://www.moviehabit.com/essay.php?story=pray02.

3. "The Scratching Is What Got Me Hooked"

1. Paul Ong and Tania Azores, "The Migration and Incorporation of Filipino Nurses," in *The New Asian Immigration on Los Angeles and Global Restructuring*, ed. Paul Ong, Edna Bonacich, and Lucie Cheng (Philadelphia: Temple University Press, 1994), 164–95. See also Catherine Choy, *Empire of Care: Nursing and Migration in Filipino American History* (Durham: Duke University Press, 2003); Yen Le Espiritu, *Home Bound: Filipino American Lives across Cultures, Communities, and Countries* (Berkeley: University of California Press, 2003).

2. The interviews typically took place at a café or a respondent's home.

3. Deeandroid interview, November 19, 2002.

4. Rygar interview, February 3, 2003.

5. Rey-Jun interview, January 25, 2002.

6. Statistix interview, October 22, 2002.

7. Celskiii interview, November 6, 2002.

8. Tease interview, November 26, 2002.

9. Ibid.

10. One Tyme interview, November 14, 2002.

11. Soup-a-Crunk interview, January 18, 2003.

12. Statistix interview, October 22, 2002.

13. One Tyme interview, November 14, 2002.

14. Celskiii interview, November 6, 2002.

15. Statistix interview, October 22, 2002.

16. Austin, *Taking the Train.*

17. Statistix interview, October 22, 2002.

18. Celskiii interview, November 6, 2002.

19. Rey-Jun interview, January 25, 2002.

20. Ibid.

21. Deeandroid interview, November 19, 2002.

22. Celskiii interview, November 6, 2002.

23. One Tyme interview, November 14, 2002.

24. Celskiii interview, November 6, 2002.

25. Rey-Jun interview, March 28, 2002.

26. Deeandroid interview, November 19, 2002.

27. Soup-a-Crunk interview, January 18, 2003.

28. Rey-Jun interview, January 25, 2002.

29. Statistix interview, October 22, 2002.

30. In graffiti painting, "pieces" are masterpieces involving the use of multiple colors.

31. Kai Fikentscher, *"You Better Work!" Underground Dance Music in New York City* (Hanover, N.H.: Wesleyan University Press, 2000).

32. One Tyme interview, November 14, 2002.

33. Tease interview, November 26, 2002.

34. Rygar interview, February 3, 2003.

35. Rey-Jun interview, January 25, 2002.

36. Tricia Rose, *Black Noise: Rap Music and Black Culture in Contemporary America* (Hanover, N.H.: Wesleyan University Press, 1994), 36.

37. Ibid.

38. Ibid.

39. Ibid.

40. Rygar interview, February 3, 2003.

41. Statistix interview, October 22, 2002.

42. Celskiii interview, November 6, 2002.

43. Statistix interview, October 22, 2002.

44. Rygar interview, February 3, 2003.

45. One Tyme interview, November 14, 2002.

46. Rygar interview, February 3, 2003.

47. Statistix interview, October 22, 2002.

48. Celskiii interview, November 6, 2002.

49. Tease interview, November 26, 2002.

50. Statistix interview, October 22, 2002.

51. Celskiii interview, November 6, 2002.

52. This is something I will discuss in more detail in chapter 5 when I discuss the ways Pinay DJs like Celskiii reconfigure what it means to be Pinay through their involvement in DJing.

53. Deeandroid interview, November 19, 2002.

54. Rey-Jun interview, March 28, 2002.

4. "DJing as a Filipino Thing"

1. Rose, *Black Noise*; Flores, *From Bomba to Hip-hop*; Rivera, *New York Ricans*. See also Frances Negron-Muntaner, *Boricua Pop: Puerto Ricans and the Latinization of American Culture* (New York: New York University Press, 2004); Roberto P. Rodriguez-Morazzani, "Beyond the Rainbow: Mapping the Discourse on Puerto Ricans and 'Race,'" in *The Latino Studies Reader: Culture, Economy, and Society*, ed. Antonia Darder and Rodolfo D. Torres, 143–62 (Walden, Mass.: Blackwell Publishers, 1998); and Flores, "Puerto Rican and Proud."

2. Ian Maxwell, "Sydney Stylee: Hip-Hop Down Under Comin' Up," in *Global Noise: Rap and Hip-hop outside the U.S.A.*, ed. Tony Mitchell (Middletown: Wesleyan University Press, 2001), 264.

3. E. Patrick Johnson, *Appropriating Blackness: Performance and the Politics of Authenticity* (Durham: Duke University Press, 2003), 42.

4. Deeandroid interview, November 19, 2002.

5. Celskiii interview, November 6, 2002.

6. Rygar interview, February 3, 2003.

7. Rivera, *New York Ricans*, 1.

8. Flores, "Puerto Rican and Proud," 89.

9. Quoted in Deborah Wong, "The Asian American Body in Performance," in *Music and the Racial Imagination*, ed. Ronald Radano and Philip V. Bohlman (Chicago: University of Chicago Press, 2000), 80–81.

10. Soup-a-Crunk interview, January 18, 2003.

11. Shuhei Hosokawa, "Blacking Japanese: Experiencing Otherness from Afar," in *Popular Music Studies*, ed. David Hesmondhalgh and Keith Negus (New York: Oxford University Press, 2002), 224.

12. For a more detailed discussion of the idealization of the "old school," see Kembrew McLeod, "Authenticity within Hip-hop and Other Cultures Threatened with Assimilation," *Journal of Communication* 49, no. 4 (1999): 134–50.

13. Crisell, White, and Principe, *On the Record,* 141.

14. Hans Weisethaunet and Ulf Lindberg, "Authenticity Revisited: The Rock Critic and the Changing Real," *Popular Music and Society* 33, no. 4 (2010): 469.

15. Soup-a-Crunk interview, January 18, 2003.

16. One Tyme interview, November 14, 2002.

17. David Hesmondhalgh and Caspar Melville, "Urban Breakbeat Culture: Repercussions of Hip-hop in the United Kingdom," in Mitchell, *Global Noise,* 98.

18. Ibid., 98.

19. Brian Currid, "'We Are Family': House Music and Queer Performativity," in *Cruising the Performative: Interventions into the Representations of Ethnicity, Nationality, and Sexuality,* ed. Sue-Ellen Case, Philip Brett, and Susan Leigh Foster (Bloomington: Indiana University Press, 1995), 184.

20. Rey-Jun interview, March 28, 2002.

21. Quoted in Pisares, "Do You Mis(recognize) Me," 174.

22. One Tyme interview, November 14, 2002.

23. Rey-Jun interview, March 28, 2002.

24. Rey-Jun's comments resonate with those of Martin F. Manalansan IV's respondents, Filipino gay men who do not relate to other Asians or to an Asian identity and conceptualize "Asia" or "Asian" only in geographic terms. Like Rey-Jun, they believe that substantial differences exist between Filipinos and other Asian groups that render the category "Asian American" problematic. See Martin F. Manalansan IV, *Global Divas: Filipino Gay Men in the Diaspora* (Durham: Duke University Press, 2003).

25. Pisares, "Do You Mis(recognize) Me," 174.

26. See, for example, Antonio T. Tiongson Jr., "On Filipinos, Filipino Americans, and U.S. Imperialism: Interview with Oscar V. Campomanes," in *Positively No Filipinos Allowed: Building Communities and Discourse,* ed. Antonio T. Tiongson Jr., Edgardo V. Gutierrez, and Ricardo V. Gutierrez (Philadelphia: Temple University Press), 26–42.

27. Elizabeth H. Pisares, "Daly City Is My Nation: Race, Imperialism and the Claiming of Pinay/Pinoy identities in Filipino American Culture" (PhD diss., University of California, Berkeley, 1999).

28. Quoted in ibid., 147.

29. See Pisares, "Do You Mis(recognize) Me."

30. Quoted in Ronald Pineda, "Spin Control," *Filipinas,* May 1998, 30.

31. Pisares, "Do You Mis(recognize) Me," 194.

32. Ibid.

33. Juliana Snapper, "Scratching the Surface: Spinning Time and Identity in Hip-hop Turntablism," *European Journal of Cultural Studies* 7, no. 1 (2004): 19.

34. Leti Volpp makes a similar point in relation to her nuanced discussion of the depoliticizing effects of cultural discourse in "Blaming Culture for Bad Behavior," *Yale*

Journal of Law and the Humanities 12, no. 89 (2000): 89–116. See also Leti Volpp, "(Mis)Identifying Culture: Asian Women and the 'Cultural Defense,'" in *Asian American Studies: A Reader*, ed. Jean Yu-wen Shen Wu and Min Song, 391–422 (New Brunswick: Rutgers University Press, 2000).

35. Anita Mannur, "Model Minorities Can Cook: Fusion Cuisine in Asian America," in *East Main Street: Asian American Popular Culture*, ed. Shilpa Dave, LeiLani Nishime, and Tasha G. Oren (New York: New York University Press, 2005), 86.

36. Dominguez, "Invoking Culture," 32.

37. Stuart Hall, "What Is This 'Black' in Black Popular Culture?," in *Black Popular Culture*, ed. Gina Dent (Seattle: Bay Press, 1992), 23.

38. Rodriguez, *Suspended Apocalypse*, 34.

39. Ibid., 90.

40. Ibid., 35.

41. Celskiii interview, November 6, 2002.

42. Rey-Jun interview, March 28, 2002.

43. It has become a fairly standard move among contemporary cultural critics to, in an effort to provide a more complex understanding of culture, posit the plurality or impossibility of identifying a specific point of origin, a move deemed as essentialist. These same critics point to the syncretic character of cultural forces, yet they leave undertheorized the politics at stake, and how this kind of claim is easily recuperated by liberal pluralist discourse. See Gilroy, *The Black Atlantic*.

5. The Normative Boundaries of Filipinoness

1. Sarah Thornton, *Club Cultures: Music, Media and Subcultural Capital* (Hanover, N.H.: Wesleyan University Press, 1996).

2. Yen Le Espiritu, "The Intersection of Race, Ethnicity, and Class: The Multiple Identities of Second-Generation Filipinos," in *Second Generation: Ethnic Identity among Asian Americans*, ed. Pyong Gap Min (Walnut Creek, Calif.: Altamira Press, 2002), 33.

3. Gonzalves, *The Day the Dancers Stayed*.

4. Stuart Hall, "Cultural Identity and Diaspora," in *Theorizing Diaspora: A Reader*, ed. Jana Evans Braziel and Anita Mannur (Malden, Mass.: Blackwell, 2003), 236.

5. Gopinath, "'Bombay, U.K., Yuba City,'" 317.

6. Gilroy, *The Black Atlantic*, 86.

7. Soup-a-Crunk interview, January 18, 2003.

8. See, for example, Tony Langlois, "Can You Feel It? DJs and House Music Culture in the UK," *Popular Music* 11, no. 2 (1992): 229–38. For a more general discussion of the ascendancy of DJs in popular culture, see Bill Brewster and Frank Broughton, *Last Night a DJ Saved My Life: The History of the Disc Jockey* (New York: Grove Press, 2000); Reighley, *Looking for the Perfect Beat*; and Poschardt, *DJ Culture*. In many ways, the proliferation of literature on DJs is a reflection of the increasing popularity of DJs. For the most part, however, these accounts are largely descriptive and celebratory, providing little or no analysis.

9. Soup-a-Crunk interview, January 18, 2003.

10. For a consideration of the masculinist orientation of rock, see Simon Frith and Angela McRobbie, "Rock and Sexuality," in *On Record: Rock, Pop, and the Written Word,* ed. Simon Frith and Andrew Goodwin, 317–32 (New York: Routledge, 1990).

11. Steve Waksman is actually referring to the electric guitar, but I find his comments relevant to the ways Filipino DJs make use of turntables. See Waksman, "Black Sound, Black Body: Jimi Hendrix, the Electric Guitar, and the Meanings of Blackness," *Popular Music and Society* 23, no. 1 (1999): 104.

12. Reighley, *Looking for the Perfect Beat,* 177.

13. See, for example, Nazli Kibria, *Family Tightrope: The Changing Lives of Vietnamese Americans* (Princeton: Princeton University Press, 1993); Pierette Hondagneu-Sotelo, *Gendered Transitions: Mexican Experiences of Immigration* (Berkeley: University of California Press, 1994); and a special issue of the *American Behavioral Scientist* 42, no. 4 (1999) that focuses on gender and migration, with contributions from feminist scholars like Pierette Hondagneu-Sotelo, Patricia R. Pessar, and Yen Le Espiritu. See also Espiritu, *Home Bound.*

14. Espiritu, *Home Bound,* 131.

15. In the case of Filipino men in the U.S. Navy, for instance, enlisting has contradictory effects, undermining their masculinity in the United States but bolstering it "back home" in the form of monetary support to family and friends and the accumulation of material goods. See Espiritu, *Home Bound,* 127–56.

16. Linda N. Espana-Maram makes this point in relation to taxi dance halls and how they enabled Filipino workers to redefine the meanings attached to brown bodies—as sources of enjoyment, style, and sensuality rather than as exploitable working bodies ideally suited to engage in stoop labor. In many ways, therefore, DJ culture operates in analogous ways to dance halls of the 1920s and 1930s. See Linda Espana-Maram, *Creating Masculinity in Los Angeles's Little Manila : Working-Class Filipinos and Popular Culture, 1920s–1950s* (New York: Columbia University Press, 2006). See also Lucy Mae San Pablo Burn's essay "'Splendid Dancing': Filipino 'Exceptionalism' in Taxi Dancehalls," *Dance Research Journal* 40, no. 2 (2008): 23–40, which focuses on the signification of the Filipino dancing body in relation to the discourse of exceptionality that served to sanction U.S. imperial policy.

17. Rygar interview, February 3, 2003.

18. Celskiii interview, November 6, 2002.

19. One Tyme interview, November 14, 2002.

20. Celskiii interview, November 6, 2002.

21. One Tyme interview, November 14, 2002.

22. A similar dynamic operates in other genres of music like rock. See Mavis Bayton, "Women and the Electric Guitar," in *Sexing the Groove: Popular Music and Gender,* ed. Sheila Whiteley, 37–49 (New York: Routledge, 1997).

23. Rey-Jun interview, March 28, 2002.

24. One Tyme interview, November 14, 2002.

25. This is similar to the way female youth are evaluated in the other elements of hip-hop. In her analysis of hip-hop music videos, for example, Rana A. Emerson shows that black women are depicted primarily as eye candy, which serves to undermine their legitimacy as artists. See Rana A. Emerson, "'Where My Girls At?' Negotiating Black Womanhood in Music Videos," *Gender and Society* 16, no. 1 (2002): 115–32. For a discussion of the sexualization of female youth in graffiti, see Nancy Macdonald, *The Graffiti Subculture: Youth, Masculinity, and Identity in London and New York* (New York: Palgrave, 2001).

26. Rey-Jun interview, March 28, 2002.

27. Tease interview, November 11, 2002.

28. This kind of thinking is in line with what Lisa A. Lewis calls the ideology of sexual favors that has characterized music culture and history and that has functioned to invalidate female musicianship. For a more detailed discussion, see Lisa A. Lewis, *Gender Politics and MTV: Voicing the Difference* (Philadelphia: Temple University Press, 1990).

29. One Tyme interview, November 14, 2002.

30. Celskiii interview, November 6, 2002.

31. Ibid.

32. Ibid.

33. Tease interview, November 11, 2002.

34. This resonates with the long history of coding of musical instruments as masculine or feminine. See Julia Eklund Koza, "Music and the Feminine Sphere: Images of Women as Musicians in Godey's Lady's Book, 1830–1877," *Music Quarterly* 75, no. 2 (1991): 103–29.

35. Celskiii interview, November 6, 2002.

36. Ibid.

37. Ibid.

38. Deeandroid interview, November 19, 2002.

39. See, for example, the discussion of hip-hop's deployment of fashion as a basis for identity formation in Rose, *Black Noise*, 36–40.

40. One Tyme interview, November 14, 2002.

41. Ibid.

42. Tease interview, November 11, 2002.

43. Tease interview, November 11, 2002. For a discussion of female musicians and their struggle with issues of appearance and stage presentation, see Mavis Bayton, "Feminist Musical Practice: Problems and Contradictions," in *Rock and Popular Music: Politics, Policies, Institutions*, ed. Tony Bennett, Simon Frith, Lawrence Grossberg, John Sheperd, and Graeme Turner, 177–92 (London: Routledge, 1993).

44. In the realm of MCing, a similar dynamic takes place. See, for example, Perry, *Prophets of the Hood*; Jason D. Haugen, "'Unladylike Divas': Language, Gender and Female Gangsta Rappers," *Popular Music and Society* 26 (2003): 429–44.

45. One Tyme interview, November 14, 2002.

46. Ibid.

47. Celskiii interview, November 6, 2002.

48. Mendoza-Denton focuses on articulations of a specific kind of femininity among Latina gang members that revolves around the use of makeup. See Norma Mendoza-Denton, "'Muy Macha': Gender and Ideology in Gang-Girls' Discourse about Makeup," *Ethnos* 61, no. 1–2 (1996): 48.

49. Rosa Linda Fregoso, "Re-Imagining Chicana Urban Identities in the Public Sphere, *Cool Chula Style*," in *Between Woman and Nation: Nationalism, Transnational Feminisms, and the State*, ed. Caren Kaplan, Norma Alarcon, and Minoo Moallem (Durham: Duke University Press, 1999), 78.

Conclusion

1. Halifu Osumare, *The Africanist Aesthetic in Global Hip-hop: Power Moves* (New York: Palgrave Macmillan, 2008); Russell A. Potter, *Spectacular Vernaculars: Hip-hop and the Politics of Postmodernism* (Albany: State University of New York Press, 1995); Vergara, *Pinoy Capital*.

2. Hosokawa, "Blacking Japanese," 223–37; David Grazian, *Blue Chicago: The Search for Authenticity in Urban Blues Clubs* (Chicago: University of Chicago Press, 2005).

3. *Planet B-Boy*, directed by Benson Lee (New York: Arts Alliance America, 2008), DVD.

4. Ibid.

5. Ibid.

6. Jared A. Ball, *I Mix What I Like: A Mixtape Manifesto* (Oakland, Calif.: AK Press, 2011). I would like to thank Shannon Mason for directing my attention to this text.

7. Alan Tomlinson identifies a similar dynamic when it comes to the Olympics in his "Olympic Spectacle: Opening Ceremonies and Some Paradoxes of Globalization," *Media, Culture and Society* 18 (1996): 583–602.

8. Anne McClintock, *Imperial Leather: Race, Gender, and Sexuality in the Colonial Context* (New York: Routledge, 1995), 353.

9. Ibid., 354.

10. Aniko Imre, "Hip-hop Nation and Gender Politics," *Thamyris/Intersecting* 18 (2007): 267.

11. Roger Rouse, "Thinking through Transnationalism: Notes on the Cultural Politics of Class Relations in the Contemporary United States," *Public Culture* 7 (1995): 380.

12. Arjun Appadurai, "Disjuncture and Difference in the Global Cultural Economy," *Public Culture* 2, no. 2 (1990): 1–24. See also Stuart Hall, "The Question of Cultural Identity," in *Modernity: An Introduction to Modern Societies*, ed. Stuart Hall, David Held, Don Hubbert, and Kenneth Thompson, 595–634 (Cambridge, Mass.: Polity Press, 1996).

13. Neil Strauss, "A Land with Rhythm and Beats for All," *New York Times*, August 22, 1999, AR28.

14. Ibid.

15. Ibid., AR29.

16. Maxwell, "Sydney Stylee," 271.

17. Imre, "Hip-hop Nation and Gender Politics," 267.

18. Heath, "True Heads," 848.

19. Devitt, "Lost in Translation," 128.

20. Osumare, *The Africanist Aesthetic*, 11.

21. Oneka LaBennett, *She's Mad Real: Popular Culture and West Indian Girls in Brooklyn* (New York: New York University Press, 2011).

22. Toure, "In the End, Black Men Must Lead," *New York Times*, August 22, 1999, AR1.

23. Ibid.

24. Ibid., AR1, AR28.

25. Cheryl L. Keyes, *Rap Music and Street Consciousness* (Urbana: University of Illinois Press, 2002), 157.

26. Ibid.

27. Alim, "Hip-hop Nation Language," 394.

28. H. Samy Alim, "Street Conscious Copula Variation in the Hip-hop Nation," *American Speech* 77, no. 3 (2002): 290.

29. Jeffrey Louis Decker, "The State of Rap: Time and Place in Hip-hop Nationalism," *Social Text* 34 (1993): 59.

30. Ibid., 54.

31. Charise L. Cheney, *Brothers Gonna Work It Out: Sexual Politics in the Golden Age of Rap Nationalism* (New York: New York University Press, 2005), 173.

32. Decker, "The State of Rap," 72.

33. Cheney, *Brothers Gonna Work It Out*, 171.

34. LaBennett, *She's Mad Real*, 103–33.

35. Heath, "True Heads," 849.

36. Ibid., 863.

37. Ibid., 864.

38. McClintock, *Imperial Leather*; Anne McClintock, Aamir Mufti, and Ella Shohat, eds. *Dangerous Liaisons: Gender, Nation, and Postcolonial Perspectives* (Minneapolis: University of Minnesota Press, 1997).

39. See, for example, Gayatri Gopinath, *Impossible Desires: Queer Diasporas and South Asian Public Cultures* (Durham: Duke University Press, 2005).

40. Rodriguez, *Suspended Apocalypse*, 33–34.

41. See *The Decolonized Eye*.

42. Gonzalves, *The Day the Dancers Stayed*, 12.

43. *Scratch*.

44. Heath, "True Heads," 864.

Index

Unless otherwise noted, topics refer to U.S.-based Filipinos. Notes are listed as *n* or *ns* for a single or multiple notes on a page.

Vergara, Benito M., 89
Village Voice, 89
Volpp, Leti, 114n34
VULCAN (graffiti artist), 25

Waksman, Steve, 71, 115n11
Wanted (graffiti group), 23
Watkins, S. Craig, *Hip-Hop Matters*, 1
Weisethaunet, Hans, and Ulf Lindberg, 54
West Indian female youth, 98
West Indian influences in hip-hop, 3
white rappers and MCs, 21–22,
　109n14

white supremacy, 100
Wild Style (film), 26
writing: graffiti writing, 4–5, 11,
　24, 109n22, 111n30, 116n25;
　a multiracial expressive form,
　21–26
writing culture, 24–25, 109n22

youth identity, 11–12. *See also* U.S.-
　based Filipino youth

Z-Trip, 54

Antonio T. Tiongson Jr. is assistant professor of American studies at the University of New Mexico. He is coeditor of the anthology *Positively No Filipinos Allowed: Building Communities and Discourse* (2006). His research interests include youth cultural politics, comparative racializations, and empire.